Gazing Upon Eternity

A Call to Be Saints
Through Mystical Reflections

Conor McCourt

Copyright © 2024 by Conor McCourt

Gazing Upon Eternity
A Collection of Mystical Musings

All rights reserved.
No part of this work may be used or reproduced, transmitted, stored, or used in any form or by any means graphic, electronic, or mechanical, including but not limited to photocopying, recording, scanning, digitizing, taping, Web distribution, information networks or information storage and retrieval systems, or in any manner whatsoever without prior written permission from the publisher. In this world of digital information and rapidly changing technology, some citations do not provide exact page numbers or credit the original source. We regret any errors, which are a result of the ease with which we consume information.

"He Desired Me So I Came Close," from the Penguin publication Love Poems from God: Twelve Sacred Voices from the East and West by Daniel Ladinsky © 2002 and used with permission.
www.danielladinsky.com.

Edited by Laurie Knight
Cover Design by: Kristina Edstrom

An Imprint for GracePoint Publishing
(www.GracePointPublishing.com)

GracePoint Matrix, LLC
624 S. Cascade Ave, Suite 201
Colorado Springs, CO 80903
www.GracePointMatrix.com
Email: Admin@GracePointMatrix.com
SAN # 991-6032

Library of Congress Control Number: 2024938240

ISBN: (Paperback) 978-1-961347-62-5
eISBN: 978-1-961347-61-8

Books may be purchased for educational, business, or sales promotional use.
For bulk order requests and price schedule contact:
Orders@GracePointPublishing.com

Table of Contents

ACKNOWLEDGMENT v
FOREWORD vii
   Called to Be Saints 1
   Influenced by Saints 5
   A Soul's Desire 7
   A Contemplative Soul 9
   Seeking in All Weather 13
   In the Fortress of Peace 15
   A Formless Love 19
   Renewed by Night 21
   The Gift of Grace 23
   Captured by Love 25
   A Day in the Life 27
   The Topography of the Heart 29
   A Healing Love 31
   Touched by Grace 33

A Trusting Surrender 35
The Twilight of Abandonment 37
The Celestial Shore 39
A Heart Longing 41
The Ascending Path 43
A Return to Love 46
My Hidden Companion 48
Emanations of a Soul 51
Remain in Me 53
Perseverance in Prayer 55
Calico Skies 58
Seeking the Seeker 60
Heart Letters 64
The Consolation of Love 66
Renewed by Change 69
The Fragrance of Prayer 71
The Advancement of Light 74
Go Beyond in Silence 76
A Divine Gesture 78
A Love Unknown 80
The Topography of a Veiled Heart 83
The Place of Refuge 85
Life's Pendulum 88

The Interior Battlefield 91

A Living Faith 94

A Thoughtless Prayer 96

A Personal Cross 99

The Way of Humility 102

A Brighter Courage 106

An Ever-New Love 109

A Devotional Air 111

Think of Me 113

The Inner Chamber 116

Timeless Patience 120

God Speaks to Souls 123

Resting on Your Heart 128

ABOUT THE AUTHOR 131

RESOURCES 133

All quotes are from internet sites like Catholic Storeroom, BrainyQuotes, or AZ Quotes, and can be easily searched, unless otherwise noted.

Blessed are they that enter far into inward things and endeavour to prepare themselves, more and more, by daily exercises, for the receiving of heavenly secrets.

St. Thomas à Kempis

Dedicated to all seeking hearts.

We are all one soul, in whom God dwells. As we live together seeking virtue, we may be scattered lights throughout the world carried within different clouds, and although we may never physically meet, we are drawn together as pilgrims of peace, engineered behind the veil by threads of Divine Love itself. Our works may be as different as the streets we walk upon, but despite our external differences we live together, abiding within the same Spirit, who calls us Her very own.

My Love, imprint upon the hearts of those who read these humble words a pathway that will lead them back to Thee. And rest, lovingly cradled in the hearts of all souls as you seek to convey your sweet fragrance to those that yearn for your guiding Presence.

Amen.

~

They can be like the sun, words.

They can do for the heart what light can for a field.

St. John of the Cross

~

This book is dedicated to my parents, Sean and Eileen, to my children, and to those dear happy souls who brought love and support to my life.

ACKNOWLEDGMENT

I would like to sincerely thank my early formless spiritual teachers, especially Father Anthony De Mello for helping me see life from a different perspective and through a wider vision. Also, I want to thank my saintly companions that Spirit guided me toward: St. Teresa of Avila, St. Francis de Sales, and St. Therese of Lisieux whose infused guidance played a significant, inspiring role in my contemplative writing. I always felt their presence close to me during the process of writing *Gazing Upon Eternity* as my prayers never went unheard whenever I sought inspiration from Spirit and the saints.

Many thanks to the staff of the Armagh Robinson Library, who always made me feel so welcome to study and write within the inspiring and elegant eighteenth-century Georgian setting of one of Ireland's oldest public libraries.

Also, I would like to thank the members of my contemplative Facebook groups Soul Whispers and Contemplative Souls, who supported my writings and reflections and encouraged me to produce a book.

Thank you to my late parents, Sean and Eileen, whose unseen but felt love and support have always surrounded me.

This book is dedicated to the brave souls who tread the narrow way and persevere therein.

We are all one soul, in whom God dwells, connected as one soul through seeking virtue. We may be scattered lights throughout the world, carried within different clouds and although we may never meet on this physical realm, we are drawn together as pilgrims of peace on our route, though each is distinctly different, back home to the Divine. Through and with the guidance of Spirit, we are all enveloped and called upon as His very own.

FOREWORD

There is a deeply sacred space within us all, located deep within the soul. It is the great mystery of the Divine and whether we are aware of it or not, I believe it is constantly loving us, reaching for us, calling for us to turn towards It, to be in communion with It.

In the writings and poetry of all the great mystics and poets they tell us the path to this communion is through the heart, our heart. Our open heart, our surrendered heart, our yearning heart. The path seems to originate within, and at the same time, is through our own hearts. It's as if the Divine reaches out through our own unique heart, with all its clarities and confusions, holds us in Its loving grasp, and then gently draws us back through our heart to merge with the heart of the Divine.

This is a path of devotion, prayer, and contemplation. It is a journey of opening to the sacred and then allowing it to change you, to work its magic upon you and through you.

In these times of unlimited distractions, it can be hard to wrap one's mind around the notion of simply being in contemplation. Yet few things are more needed in helping us find the inner spiritual treasures of this life. Contemplation can be invaluable in helping us realize our true nature and our relationship with the Divine.

There is an art to contemplation. It is not merely an intellectual process that carries you to some new concept. There is also a deep opening of the heart, like an offering of oneself to the Divine mysteries that exist beyond the intellect and then allowing what comes forward to change you. The journey of mystical contemplation is a deeply personal one that will impact all areas of your life and change how you move through the world.

This brings me to the work of Conor McCourt, a contemporary mystical contemplative writer. His uncanny ability to articulate the nuances of the devotional path to the Divine Beloved is deeply inspiring. As you read the heart offerings in this beautiful book, I think you will feel, as I have, the depth of his own experiences coupled with his profound desire to share the joy of the contemplative path to God.

Let this book guide you, inspire you, and be your companion as you find your way through your precious, open heart to the Divine Beloved within us all.

David Cronin
Writer and photographer

Called to Be Saints

"The righteous themselves know but in part; they are too weak of sight to behold all that God is doing with them; they know that they have received a great gift from Him; that they have powers, and capacities, and sympathies, and an energy derived from the Infinite and Eternal; that wisdom, and love, and mercy and purity, have no measure or limit, except the nature in which they dwell; as the powers of seeing or of knowing are limited only by the organisation of the body, and the conditions by which we attain to knowledge: and yet, with this teeming consciousness, the secret of their regeneration is not half known, even by themselves; they cannot comprehend it, because they are comprehended by it, as a thing that is greater than they; and in it they have their being; and nevertheless, as, on the one side they are baffled by the greatness of the gift, so on the other, are they straitened by the littleness of their own finite capacities. They feel themselves beset by earthly tempers, and narrow thoughts, and shadows which fall inwardly upon their hearts, and to their own eyes they seem to be of a dim and earthly nature; they know of themselves far more evil than good; the visible and prominent points of their own character are the darker lines, and the gloomier spots which lie upon the surface; in their own sight they have no brightness, or, at the best, a pale sickly light, often overcast; and they ask, 'Can this be the gift of righteousness? Can this swerving will, and faint striving, and ready yielding, and often slumbering, and all this throng of hasty tempers, and high thoughts, and unchastened imaginations, can all this dwell in the soul of the righteous?...' And how must all this perplexity be multiplied when a righteous man falls, be it never so little, from his obedience; when to the abiding sense of inward evil is added the consciousness of fresh transgression!... From all this we may see what is the hiddenness of our spiritual life—how little it is perceived and understood by others—how imperfectly it is apprehended even by ourselves—how it may be for a time, as it were, altogether hidden from our own eyes; and yet we feel within us some thing which prophesies of our lot in God's Kingdom, and foretels the perfection of our being here after; we feel something which pledges to us that we shall not fall back again to the dominion of unrighteousness; something which assures us that we shall not be for ever bounded by the limits of imperfection; we feel yearnings, and aspirations, and breathing hopes, and conscious energies, which reach after a larger sphere of being. And so it shall be; for 'the righteous shall shine forth as the sun in the kingdom of their Father'" (Manning, 1850, 16).

"The saints have no need of honor from us; neither does our devotion add the slightest thing to what is theirs. Clearly, if we venerate their memory, it serves us, not them. But I tell you, when I think of them, I feel myself inflamed by a tremendous yearning.

"Calling the saints to mind inspires, or rather arouses in us, above all else, a longing to enjoy their company, so desirable in itself. We long to share in the citizenship of heaven, to dwell with the spirits of the blessed, to join the assembly of patriarchs, the ranks of the prophets, the council of apostles, the great host of martyrs, the noble company of confessors and the choir of virgins. In short, we long to be united in happiness with all the saints. But our dispositions change. ... The saints want us to be with them, and we are indifferent. The souls of the just await us, and we ignore them.

"Come... let us at length spur ourselves on. We must rise again with Christ, we must seek the world which is above and set our mind on the things of heaven. Let us long for those who are longing for us, hasten to those who are waiting for us, and ask those who look for our coming to intercede for us. We should not only want to be with the saints, we should also hope to possess their happiness. While we desire to be in their company, we must also earnestly seek to share in their glory. Do not imagine that there is anything harmful in such an ambition as this; there is no danger in setting our hearts on such glory.

"When we commemorate the saints we are inflamed with another yearning: that Christ our life may also appear to us as he appeared to them, and that we may one day share in his glory. Until then we see him not as he is, but as he became for our sake. He is our head, crowned, not with glory, but with the thorns of our sins.

"Therefore, we should aim at attaining this glory with a wholehearted and prudent desire. That we may rightly hope and strive for such blessedness, we must above all seek the prayers of the saints. Thus, what is beyond our own powers to obtain will be granted through their intercession."

~ St. Bernard of Clairvaux

Cite: All quotes come from The Catholic Storeroom online unless otherwise noted.

Influenced by Saints

"The devotional language of saints is very much relevant to the modern-day pilgrim. Like trees they offer shelter from the storms of life. Their interior understanding is just like a tree, deeply rooted, producing good fruit through virtue, and yet whose teachings remain undisturbed by the winds of change. Saints and mystics have both influenced and inspired my life and writings, especially those of St. Therese of Lisieux and St. Francis de Sales who both have left an imprint on my heart. Not only are their teachings relevant, but they are also very reliable and accessible for modern spiritual living. Henri Nouwen writes, 'They are men and women like, us who live ordinary lives and struggle with ordinary problems. What makes them saints is their clear and unwavering focus on God and God's people.'" Only a loving thought and a thin veil separate us. They remain close.

St. Thomas Aquinas writes, "'The greater the charity of the Saints in their heavenly home, the more they intercede for those who are still on their journey, and the more they can help them by their prayers, the more they are united with God, the more effective those prayers are. This is in accordance with Divine order, which makes higher things react upon lower things like the brightness of the sun filling the atmosphere.' The saints are the uplifters of souls. Their inexhaustible energy is omnipotent, inspiring, and delightful. Saint Bernard of Clairvaux, referring to saints, writes, 'When I think of them, I feel myself inflamed by tremendous yearning.' God invites us to become saints because those who follow them will become saints. We must strive to place our confidence and gaze, like saints, on the eternal light that flickers undisturbed by the tumult of life."

Conor McCourt, February 2023

A Soul's Desire

No matter the thoughts of your mind or the perceptions which are formulated by the experiences of your life, it is the soul's longing that attracts God's grace. The soul's natural magnetic pull to Spirit makes us intuitively aware of a different level of consciousness. Our natural appetite hungers for Divine love. A soul stirred with this internal delight experiences an inner joy void of mental or sensory input and the security of a central knowing of soul union with Spirit. This felt power within you ignites life and motivates you in many ways. Many people often do not recognize this because their minds are buried in the debris of emotional suffering and the perceptions of the material mind. The soul is thus lost, covered up by many layers that encase the soul's natural expressiveness. It takes effort to go beyond the mechanics of the mind to that place of understanding and soul awareness. But if you seek God willingly and sincerely, connecting mind to heart, heart to soul, and soul to Spirit, you will feel a love. It's not a human natural love, but a love with the essence of Heaven. Many hidden paths will appear for you. A deeper understanding will come to you; many of your unanswered questions will be answered, and with concerted effort and longing, you will experience a oneness, a presence of God within you. Don't let mental machinations obscure your soul's vision in life. Rely on the strength of your soul, which is anchored firmly with God alone. At the beginning of your spiritual path, the pendulum of temporal matter and soul will go back and forth from the sense of joy experienced through the soul to the confusion of life. In time, the pendulum will swing less and less until you are rooted in your soul's perceptions and a deeper knowing. Be nurtured by this inherent truth despite the turbulence of life. Refuse to be whisked away by its unruly transport, despite its grip upon your heart. Remain rooted steadfast in the truth that God dwells within your most tenderest self, seeking your heart.

A Contemplative Soul

The pursuit of the contemplative life is something for which a great and sustained effort on the part of the powers of the soul is required, an effort to rise from earthly to heavenly things, an effort to keep one's attention fixed on spiritual things, an effort to pass beyond and above the sphere of things visible to the eyes of flesh, an effort finally to hem oneself in, so to speak, in order to gain access to spaces that are broad and open. There are times indeed when one succeeds, overcoming the opposing obscureity of one's blindness and catching at least a glimpse, be it ever so fleeting and superficial, of boundless light.

~ St. Gregory the Great

Beloved, despite our incompleteness, You remain with us, concealed in the little heaven of our souls. We tread unknowingly yet lightly along this rugged path of life with our hearts gazing upon your hidden mystery, ignited by the thought of You—a devotional gesture, a flicker of grace, a fleeting glimpse, a light within light. Even when the flame of our prayer dims, You are there, unchanged amid the temporal currents of mindful narratives, loving us more just so we can love and find our way back to You.

Henri Nouwen writes, "Being useless and silent in the presence of our God belongs to the core of all prayer. In the beginning we often hear our own unruly inner noises more loudly than God's voice. This is at times very hard to tolerate. But slowly, very slowly, we discover that the silent time makes us quiet and deepens our awareness of ourselves and God. Then, very soon, we start missing these moments when we are deprived of them, and before we are fully aware of it an inner momentum has developed that draws us more and more into silence and closer to that still point where God speaks to us" (Nouwen 1986, 130).

The Beloved conveys Her voiceless sermons in waves of intuitive feelings, free from the stamp of egoic interpretation. For the mind with all its fullness cannot reenact such a divine gesture of grace. St. Teresa of Avila encourages us to form the habit of looking at nothing and staying in no place which will distract these outward senses. May we be sure that they are walking on an excellent road and will come without fail to drink the living water of the fountain.

St. Albert the Great writes, "Furthermore, while the soul is withdrawn from everything and is turned within, the eye of contemplation is opened and sets itself up a ladder by which it can pass to the contemplation of God. By this contemplation the soul is set on fire for eternal things by the heavenly and divine good things it experiences, and views all the things of time from a distance and as if they were nothing."

God is love and infinitely gentle to the heart, a forever companion who guides and encourages us to bravely pierce through the layers that veil the soul from His mirrored image. Contemplation is resting with God in silent devotion. The noise of intellectual activity ceases as time seems to pause past memory and future plan as the heart rests momentarily from the world's dim glare. By the recollection of the senses in silent prayer, we retire inwardly where God dwells as we draw each other near.

St. Teresa of Avila writes, "Contemplative prayer in my opinion is nothing else than a close sharing between friends; it means taking time frequently to be alone with him who we know loves us." In prayer, we must simply allow ourselves to be loved despite the feelings of our incompleteness. Arrive openly, for the Beloved knows your heart's desire.

St. Francis de Sales writes, "If the heart wanders or is distracted, bring it back to the point quite gently and replace it tenderly in its Master's presence. And even if you did nothing during the whole of your hour but bring your heart back and place it again in Our Lord's presence, though it went away every time you brought it back, your hour would be very well employed."

Be gentle with yourself. Whenever thoughts arise in prayer, remember not to serve them a cup of tea. Remain separate from the thinker, for it is not your nature. St. Clement Hofbauer advises us to think of thoughts as little as we do of the leaves that fall from trees and not to dwell on them. St. Thomas Aquinas writes, "A heart which is free from thoughts and affections alien to God is like a temple consecrated to the Lord, in which we can contemplate him even in this world." As our contemplation deepens through the gift of grace, we begin to listen less to the mental narrative and listen more attentively to God. No longer will thoughts hold their mindful dominance as the mind ascends towards the heart along the ancient highway where saints and mystics have trod.

Seeking in All Weather

Dear souls that seek to walk in security and comfort in spiritual things: If you knew just how necessary it is to suffer and to endure in order to reach such a lofty state of security and consolation… then you would in no way seek consolation, either from God or from creatures.

~ St. John of the Cross

There is a mystical saying that goes "Seek the God of consolations and not the consolations of God." The Divine bestows spiritual gifts upon a soul who seeks to mirror its very own image. St. Augustine writes, "when we know God, some likeness of God is made in us."

Interior peace and an intuitive understanding are usually the first gifts of God's consolations to visit the port of an awakening heart. It is important to visualize the love and source behind the gift instead of being engaged fully within the consolation itself. The content of our devotional heart invites God to enter our lives, for Spirit cannot resist the love that emanates from a veiled human soul that longs for unification with its indwelling Host. Upon the spiritual way we are truly directionless, for God is the great conductor of our lives, and the seeker to experience the Divine mystery must abandon all their incompleteness and aspirations into the firmament of God's Love.

Spirit visits our hearts in many sacred ways. Maybe an unexpected rapture ripples a celestial warmth throughout the body, or God may lead us through the parched desert of our hearts to enable us to seek the strength of light through the twilight of abandonment. The Divine knows which unique route is most beneficial for the development of our souls. Look at the lives of the great saints. St. Teresa of Avila was blessed with many raptures throughout her mystical life. St. Padre Pio, on the other hand, felt the Love of the formless Christ more abundantly in times of great trials. He wrote, "O what precious moments these are. It is a happiness that the Lord gives me to relish almost always in moments of affliction. At these moments, more than ever, when the whole world troubles and weighs on me, I desire nothing other than to love and to suffer. Yes, my Father, even amid so much suffering, I am happy because it seems as if my heart is beating with Jesus' heart."

In the Fortress of Peace

For until I am one with him I can never have true rest nor peace. I can never know it until I am held so close to him that there is nothing in between.

~ St. Julian of Norwich

My Beloved, through the humility of a veiled heart, we seek Your Grace, for the aroma of Your peace permeates through each open portal of our soul's desires for advancing union. In the stillness of Your peace, all feeling of incompleteness evaporates by the gentle balm of Your intimate gentleness as clouds of self-doubt disperse that previously sought the preciousness of our uniqueness.

Lord, may the celestial dew rain its peace upon our devotion as the fragrant salve of Your essence washes over the formless expanse of all hearts, wherein each soul You dwell, hidden by veils but yet felt through vision far beyond the horizon of the world's slaving glare. St. Francis de Sales writes, "Do not lose your inner peace for anything whatsoever, not even if your whole world seems upset. If you find that you have wandered away from the shelter of God, lead your heart back to Him quietly and simply."

Living an internalized life is the way to maintain inner peace during difficult times. Life will always test us, especially more for those who confront their sufferings in the pursuit of Divine Love. Look at the lives of the great Saints and Mystics. No matter what obstacles stood in their way, they peacefully abandoned themselves into the firmament of Love. They trusted in the secret mystery of the indwelling Spirit, but they weren't immune to suffering. They used whatever cast a shadow over their consolation as a gift to propel their hearts more deeply towards the Infinite, finding deep repose in the bleakness of visiting Winters.

St. John of the Cross writes, "The purest suffering brings with it the purest and most intimate knowledge [of God], and consequently the purest and highest joy." Retaining our peace in times of adversity patiently strengthens our vision. St. Alexis of Senaki reminds us "Everyone who loves God shows himself patient and steadfast in times of suffering. Whoever bears them bravely becomes strong and obedient to God, and whoever enters the path of following the will of God conquers his natural weakness."

Naturally, our souls seek to avoid sufferings and cleave towards divine consolations, but we can't be tested within their treasured richness. We can only flex our spiritual muscles in times of visiting hardship. The early desert Father Macarius the Great reminds us that in afflictions and sufferings, endurance and faith are concealed by the promised glory and the recovery of celestial blessings. We must contemplate the Beloved and find deep rest upon the Divine Will, where the blessing of true peace streams forth.

François Fénèlon writes, "Peace does not dwell in outward things, but within the soul; we may preserve it in the midst of the bitterest pain, if our will remains firm and submissive." The unutterable transport of peace is a reflection of the Spirit's essence working through our intellectual faculties. Usually, the felt gift of peace is one of the first consolations bestowed upon a soul. True peace is void of mental input, for it arrives at the port of the heart to be exported through the open manifolds of a new, undiluted awareness. The mind, with all its mindful potentials and striving for egoic perfection, cannot grasp or interpret such a divine harmony as an unseen infusion of peace takes root, bringing with it a celestial rhythm into the soul's iridescent center.

St. Elizabeth of the Trinity writes, "[P]raise of Glory is a soul of silence that remains like a lyre under the mysterious touch of the Holy Spirit so that He may draw from its divine harmonies." My Lord, You are the interior melody that brings the poetic essence of peace to all souls. The gentleness of your sweet ambiance radiates forth its formless fragrance upon the quietude of all seeking hearts.

A Formless Love

Live in the joy and the peace of the divine Majesty. Live lost in divine love. Live for divine love and of divine love.

~ *St. Paul of the Cross*

The essence of our being is Love. From Love we came, in Love we move, and to Love we return. Thomas à Kempis writes, "Nothing is sweeter than love, nothing more courageous, nothing higher, nothing wider, nothing more pleasant, nothing fuller nor better in Heaven and Earth: because Love is born of God, and cannot rest but in God, above all created things" (à Kempis 1878, 114).

Our true life is pervaded by the ascending Love that broadcasts from within the sacred sanctuary of the dwelling Presence. Our Divine purpose as human souls is to express Love, for God designed us to reflect Her radiant beauty. We are vehicles of Love, transported by our souls longing for unification with its veiled hidden substance.

Thomas Merton writes, "The secret of my identity is hidden in the Love and Mercy of God" (*New Seeds* 1961, 37). Our soul intuitively understands that great healing and transformations of the heart come with the further advancement into the formless Love that is always seeking us through the midst of our incompleteness. For Spirit seeks to perfume our hearts with an ethereal composition of celestial Love.

St. John of the Cross writes, "Love unites the soul with God, and, the more degrees of love the soul has, the more profoundly does it enter into God and the more it is centered in Him." Spirit transports Her essence through the compositional melodious lament of the soul. The sweet melody that ascends from the soul magnetically captures the attention of the hidden Spirit who takes great delight in the absorption of our heart in the great participation of Divine Love. God whispers to the soul through intuitive sermons of Love that nurtures and elevates our being above the falling debris of dissolving layers that once encased the soul. Open the manifolds of your spiritual heart and let Love sweep away the old clutter that once shrouded your interior treasure. Padre Pio reminds us also in the following: "[L]eave the door of your heart wide open so that he might work as he pleases."

Renewed by Night

If there be anything that is capable of setting the soul in a large place it is absolute abandonment to God. It diffuses in the soul a peace that flows like a river and the righteousness which is as the waves of the sea.

~ François Fénèlon

Spirit upon the perched terrain of my abandoned heart, I patiently wait in the bleakness of night as Your Presence departs from my devotion. Although You do not leave the port of my heart, for in truth the Creator, to be complete, cannot forsake His creation, we are an essential part of Love itself, and for Love to function, it needs to be complete in absoluteness, and each soul is an essential part of the great Lattice of Love. Even though the intuitive radio of my soul cannot reach the Eternal shore, I shall think of Thee more through the dialect and lament of my aloneness. The devotional actions we perform in spiritual dryness are more meritorious in the sight of Spirit, who always seeks to elevate and restore our hearts, especially in times of felt abandonment when all spiritual ambitions become shrouded by the twilight of hidden Love. The strength of our character is truly tested in times of aridity, for each act of devotion in dryness is seen by the Angels and Saints as a great act of virtue.

St. Teresa Benedicta of the Cross writes, "The soul may take dryness and darkness as fortunate symptoms: symptoms that God is freeing her from herself. He is disentangling her from the activity of her faculties." God manifests and transports His Love in many infinite ways, unknown through hidden visitations of Love that secretly pierce the heart beyond the horizon of all mental interpretations, as the great Celestial Physician transforms our being back into the natural state of mirrored Love. In times of spiritual dryness, be patient and compassionate with yourself. Never lose hope and abide within the healing space of the Divine mystery that is operating behind the scenes of your sensory faculties, whether in the joy of consolations or felt abandonment. Remember, God is always busy loving you, seeking you, and desires for His Love to be perceived within your formless heart.

The Gift of Grace

Grace is a certain beginning of glory in us.

~ *St. Thomas Aquinas*

My Beloved, you dwell in the space between my breath. Your gift of Grace reconstructs and cleanses my heart just so I can feel and love you more. Ven. Fulton J. Sheen writes, "As all men are touched by God's love, so all are also touched by the desire for His intimacy." It seems natural to cling to Spirit's visitations of Divine Love, but intuitive souls realise that God dispenses His transformational gift of mysteries in subtle waves as and when He pleases, either through consolations or in spiritual dryness. For God's love for us is unconditional and unchangeable despite the interior weather. During times of trials or felt abandonment (dark nights), God is testing our love for Him. Persevere with the patience of heart and never feel discouraged when Spirit retires into the iridescent depths of your being. For during such times God is purifying us, hidden from sight to ignite and render our souls to receive the abundance of greater graces. The Grace that you receive from Spirit is reflected in the sincerity of your heart, for God cannot resist the silent love that emanates from within a soul's whispering call.

Allow God's love to surge through you, for anything that is not in balance with light will be whisked away with the transformative current of celestial Love that in time will envelop each aspect of our Being, enabling us to feel little pieces of Heaven on Earth. St. Therese of Lisieux writes, "Open your heart and go direct to God. I go to that Divine Furnace to draw out life, and there my sweet Savior listens to me day and night." Arrive at the Furnace free from knowing, void of gain and complexities, for the Divine is not complicated, but gentle and inviting.

Captured by Love

Let us love the light, long to understand it and thirst after if so that led by it we may come to it, and there live for ever.

~ St. Augustine

The surrender to Love is a trusted martyrdom of the heart. The Beloved can't resist the bouquet of transcendent love that emanates from within the furnace of a surrendering heart. For God has everything except the willingness of love from an individual soul. St. Clare of Assisi writes, "We become what we love and what we love shapes what we become." Our heart is an organ of magnetic perception, celestially plumbed to seek the source of its being, which is Love itself.

To get to the root of Love is the very purpose for our human existence upon this earthly realm, for our hearts continuously seek each moment to be captured by the tender embrace of Divine Love. St. Thomas à Kempis writes, "Love is a great thing, yea, a great and thorough Good; by itself it makes everything that is heavy, light, and it bears evenly all that is uneven.

"For it carries a burden which is no burden, and makes everything that is bitter, sweet and tasteful" (*Imitation* 1878, 114).

Love is an intellectual vision unbounded by worldly afflictions. Because Love originates from Spirit, the Holy Lover of all souls, Love is eternally pure and remains undiluted by the fleeting shadows of life that can shroud the soul from expressing its inherent nature. Celestial Love bestowed upon a soul feels no strain, for it is Love that unites the soul to Spirit, the heavenly bond between creation and Creator.

A Day in the Life

Do not lose your inner peace for anything whatsoever, not even if your whole world seems upset. If you find that you have wandered away from the shelter of God, lead your heart back to Him quietly and simply.

~ St. Francis de Sales

Sufi mystic Abu Sa'id writes: "The perfect mystic is neither an ecstatic devotee lost in contemplation of Oneness, nor a saintly recluse shunning all commerce with mankind, but 'the true saint' goes in and out amongst the people and eats and sleeps with them and buys and sells in the market and marries and takes part in social intercourse, and never forgets God for a single moment." But the mystic doesn't derive their identity from society, culture, or environmental influences alone. Their true essence of Being comes from the interior Love that ascends from the interior mirror of Love itself.

The mystic wanders in steady perseverance through the desert of their hearts, piercing through clouds that shroud their way. For the mystic confronts and visions life through a different lens, undiluted by external midst. We all carry portable pieces of Heaven in the central depth of our souls. Imagine if the infinite truth of who we truly are pierced through the many veils of all misplaced hearts. Only then would the hidden fragrance of peace bloom forth, consuming the Earth. But peace firstly must begin on an individual level. Unfortunately, many souls deprive themselves of this buried treasure, for the mystic intuitively knows that without true peace there is never truly rest in oneself or towards their fellow souls.

Jewish mystic Etty Hillesum writes, "Ultimately, we have just one moral duty: to reclaim large areas of peace in ourselves, more and more peace, and to reflect it toward others. And the more peace there is in us, the more peace there will be in our troubled world" (Hillesum 1996, 218).

The Topography of the Heart

The Lord our King will hold the door of His heart open for anyone who wants to enter for an audience at any time.

~ St. Padre Pio

Listen to the sweet melody that Spirit has plumbed into your sacred depths. Allow the rhythmic pulse of adorning Love to vibrate within the mirrored reflection of your devotional heart. The spiritual heart is the perceptive mirror that visions far beyond the radio of our sensory nerves, an inexpressible experience of celestial love that transports a little Heaven into the soul. For a soul that emanates love is gifted by love itself. The spiritual heart is an unseen Paradise where the Divine choreographs the rhythmic movement of the soul's deepest desire for transformative union. Spirit, you are the healing remedy and sacred fortress to all hearts that long to feel your ethereal warmth, who, despite their veils, advance in steadfast motion, entering the narrow path that leads to the internal topography of the soul.

Karl Rahner writes, "There exists in our heart an interior land where we are alone, to which no one finds his way but God. This innermost, unfrequented chamber of our heart is really there—the only question is whether we avoid it foolishly out of guilty fear, because no one and no familiar things of this Earth can accompany us if we enter it" (Rahner, 35). The simplicity of heart draws Spirit close through the medium of its reflective content. When-ever we feel uplifted unexpectedly that is void of mental concepts or interpretation, it is then God's movement taking place within the manifolds of the soul. St. Thomas Aquinas writes, "The soul is like an uninhabited world that comes to life only when God lays His head against us."

A Healing Love

The more the soul loves, the more it desires to love, and the greater its suffering, the greater its healing.

~ St. Columbanus

Abide peacefully in the confidence that God, the Great Conductor, is orchestrating your life in celestial rhythmic harmony with great purpose and fulfilment of the Divine Love. St. Francis de Sales writes, "Let your heart then be full of courage and your courage of confidence in God, for He who gave you the first attraction of His Love will never abandon you." Beloved, your infinite Love peers out through my temporal mists, parting the clouds that cast a shadow upon the heart. Happy is the confident soul that, despite its incompleteness, can abandon at Will the weight of its cross to be embalmed by the inexpressible gift of Love that uplifts and soothes all weary hearts. Pope Francis writes, "Jesus seeks us out. He wants to heal our wounds, to soothe our feet which hurt from travelling alone, to wash each of us clean of the dust from our journey." For Spirit is the remedy and revivalist of returning hearts that taste the sweet nectar and the interior joys of Divine virtue, despite the internal pains and the pressing weight of exterior matter. St. Thomas à Kempis writes, "Grant me, O most sweet and loving Jesus, to rest in Thee, above all creatures, above all health and beauty, above all glory and honour, above all power and dignity, above all knowledge and subtilty, ... above all fame and praise, above all sweetness and comfort, above all hope and promise" (*Imitation* 1878, 152). Spirit seeks to balance and harmonise our human souls, for the spiritual heart cannot find any true peace except upon the Divine mantle of healing Love.

Touched by Grace

I know full well that the more the souls sees of God, the more it desires him, by his grace.

~ St. Julian of Norwich

The soul at its deepest centre resides far beyond the world's glare, where the impulse of surface matter becomes obscured by the lustrous veils of Eternal Love. Upon luminous terrains the soul finds its most profound repose, far from the imprint of the multitudes and earthly fretters. A soul touched by grace becomes uplifted by a momentary gift of awareness, unbounded from external patterns of sight and imagery, free from exterior influences. Grace dissolves the layers that encase and weigh the soul. Its sweet current arrives, hidden beyond sight and mental knowing.

Meister Eckhart writes, "Grace is from God, and works in the depth of the soul whose powers it employs. It is a light which issues forth to do service under the guidance of the Spirit. The Divine light permeates the soul, and lifts it above the turmoil of temporal things to rest in God. The soul cannot progress except with the light which God has given it as a nuptial gift; love works the likeness of God into the soul." A soul bestowed with Spirit's grace intuitively knows by the gift of an inward vision that this visitation of God's presence is most beneficial for spiritual growth and alignment. For God's touch upon the heart leaves an aluminous imprint that encourages the soul to seek infinitely the source of its intrinsic nature. St. Thomas Aquinas writes, "Grace is a certain beginning of glory in us. It is grace alone that draws us closer to God and strengthens our intent. For the soul must travel across mountainous terrains to find her true rest." And St. Thomas à Kempis writes: "A man must strive long and mightily within himself, before he can learn to fully master himself, and to draw his whole heart unto God" (*Imitation* 1878, 85). The gleam of God's light shines forth through our cloudiest days. For, in truth, the clamour of external life no longer holds ground over the aspirations of a soul touched by the very essence of its nature.

A Trusting Surrender

Raise up your heart after a fall, sweetly and gently, humbling yourself before God in the knowledge of your misery, and do not be astonished at your weakness, since it is not surprising that weakness should be weak, infirmity infirm, and frailty frail.

~ St. Francis de Sales

Trust in Love and don't subscribe to what the world impresses upon your tender self, for stillness and silent repose is your natural soul state. Open wide the doorway of your heart's natural perceptions and allow God to cultivate the Divine Love in You. Spirit seeks us unconditionally even before our body had taken its first breath upon this distant shore. Surrender to God the dust of a failing past that consumed the radiant beauty of the soul. St. Teresa of Calcutta writes, "Total surrender consists in giving ourselves completely to God—Why must we give ourselves fully to God? Because God has given himself to us. If God, who owes nothing to us, is ready to impart to us no less than himself, shall we answer with just a fraction of ourselves? To give ourselves fully to God is a means of receiving God Hhimself. I for God and God for me. I live for God and give up my own self, and in this way induce God to live for me. Therefore to possess God, we must allow him to possess our soul."

Play your part in life and leave the noisy clamour of the world behind the reach of your senses. Acknowledge the incompleteness of humanity's veiled heart and tread lightly upon the narrow way to love. Through the fragrance of your devotion, allow the Spirit to enter the fortress of the heart. Cultivate and cast loving seeds of devotion upon the topography of celestial grounds. The Divine feels this veiled intention and Angels take notice. As we seek to receive Divine love, all the barriers we have constructed begin to slowly thin as light penetrates through habitual clouds.

St. Nektarios of Aegina writes, "The path leading to perfection is long. Pray to God so that he will strengthen you. Patiently accept your falls and, having stood up, immediately run to God, not remaining in that place where you have fallen. Do not despair if you keep falling." The tenderest of souls carry the most wounds hidden from sight, but gentleness and strength of character radiate forth through a gentle glance of surrender.

The Twilight of Abandonment

If a man wishes to be sure of the road he treads on, he must close his eyes and walk in the dark.

~ St. John of the Cross

In the twilight of abandonment, never lose hope, for God is always busy creating new symphonies within the iridescent self. Transformational change arrives in subtle currents hidden beyond the reach of our intellectual faculties. The Divine choreographs the reconstruction of our hearts within a space free from the stamps of personal interpretation and reasoning, as our soul becomes unbound by the restraints of time and memory as it takes up the mirrored invitation to join the echoing rhymes of the Divine dance. St. Francis de Sales writes, "Our heart is made for God, and God constantly entices it and never ceases to cast before it the allurements of divine love."

There are feelings of aloneness, but we are never alone. It's the great paradox of the spiritual life. Even a single sincere thought of God in times of abandonment is a substantial act of devotion. Our strength of character is truly tested when Spirit withdraws Her presence from the soul's contemplative faculties. Hans Urs von Balthasar writes, "Every contemplative (and not only the gifted mystic), if his contemplation is an expression of living disciple-ship, must be prepared to experience the dark night to some degree. It is a sign that he is on the path of Christ, i.e., it is a sign of consolation, even though it is bound to take the form of a withdrawal of consolation." Dawn teaches us that darkness always anticipates the light, and light will always penetrate the darkness. Reginald Garrigou-Lagrange writes, "In nature, when the sun goes down and night falls, we no longer see the objects surrounding us, but we do see distant objects not visible during the day, such as the stars, which are thousands of light-years away. And the sun must hide that we may see them, that we may be able to glimpse the depths of the firmament. Analogously, during the night of the Spirit we see much farther than during the luminous period preceding it; the inferior lights must be taken away from us in order that we may begin to see the heights of the spiritual firmament." Sometimes God needs to simply move us out of the way beyond personal input to bring the soul closer in alignment with the Divine will.

The Celestial Shore

Those who are able to shut themselves up in this way within this little Heaven of the soul, wherein dwells the Maker of Heaven and earth, and who have formed the habit of looking at nothing and staying in no place which will distract these outward senses, may be sure that they are walking on an excellent road, and will come without fail to drink of the water of the fountain, for they will journey a long way in a short time. They are like one who travels in a ship, and, if he has a little good wind, reaches the end of his voyage in a few days, while those who go by land take much longer.

~ St. Teresa of Avila

In silent prayer, cast out the net of devotion towards the Eternal Shore and go far beyond the crustaceans that try to anchor the soul's natural course. Persevere therein despite the rising tides by drifting further into the tender swell of Infinite Love. Vision each unruly wave as a potential safe passage to the Eternal Island. The Beloved takes great delight in transporting shipwrecked souls back to the port of Divine Love. Thomas Merton writes, "We are carried over the sea by a ship, not by the wake of a ship. So too, what we are is to be sought in the invisible depths of our being." We must sail through life with a calmness of heart and the desire to be reconciled with our heavenly indweller. Soul, You travel alone on hidden lanes, lamped by a flicker of desiring hopes amongst barren sands.

St. Augustine writes, "For we are but travelers on a journey without as yet a fixed abode; we are on our way, not yet in our native land; we are in a state of longing, not yet of enjoyment. But let us continue on our way, and continue without sloth or respite, so that we may ultimately arrive at our destination."

A Heart Longing

Our natural will is to have God, and the good will of God is to have us, and we may never cease willing or longing for God until we have him in the fullness of joy. Christ will never have his full bliss in us until we have our full bliss in him.

~ *St. Julian of Norwich*

Despite the debris strewn across our path, it is Love alone that permeates and directs our hearts as we pilgrim through the interior vastness of infinite space, internally seeking to encompass the Divine indweller with the petals of our devotion. The intuitive soul understands by a hidden vision that God reveals Her essence equal to the reflective content of the individual heart. A single stirring of God's Love upon our lives keeps us longing for infinitely more because there is nothing else within the creative universe that can impact a heart except the felt, hidden movements of Divine Love.

The soul naturally seeks God, and God seeks out our love. St. Angela Merici writes, "God has given free will to everyone, and therefore never forces anyone—but only indicates, calls and persuades." For the multitudes are consumed by habitual clouds and cannot hear the gentle whisper that ascends through the open manifolds of an awakening soul that interiorly yearns through parting veils for a secret imprint of Grace. Have a deep longing for God within the deepest repose of the heart. St. Thomas à Kempis writes, "Who is more at rest than he who aims at nothing but God? And who more free than the man who desires nothing on earth?"

The Ascending Path

If your desire and aim is to reach the destination of the path and home of true happiness, of grace and glory, by a straight and safe way then earnestly apply your mind to seek constant purity of heart, clarity of mind and calm of the senses. Gather up your heart's desire and fix it continually on the Lord God above.

~ St. Albert the Great

Spirit, recollect our senses and lead us along the narrow ascending pathway that takes us home to the sweet ambiance of your ineffable love, where the living flame of faith reflects the inexpressible gift of your radiant gleam. The path is not stretched in narrow, smooth lanes, but runs deep through the spiralling unevenness of the soul to where an energised experience is felt beyond the glare of surface matter. Persevere therein, for the journey will take you over mountainous terrain the egoic mind would gladly seek to avoid. Remain calm and direct the heart towards the indwelling love whose gentle fragrance draws you near.

St. Nektarios of Aegina writes, "The path leading to perfection is long. Pray to God so that he will strengthen you. Patiently accept your falls, and having stood up, immediately run to God, not remaining in that place where you have fallen. Do not despair if you keep falling into your old sins. Only with the passage of time and with fervor will they be conquered. Don't let anything deprive you of hope."

On cloudy days, don't slip into hopelessness, but gently rest upon the loving thought that the Divine dwells in the deepest center of the soul, seeking you, loving You, conveying through veils the fragrance of an unseen Heaven that mysteriously keeps an uplifting beat in our hearts to persevere continually through spheres of sacredness. St. Francis de Sales writes, "Keep our eyes fixed on our Guide and upon that blessed country whither He is conducting us. What should it matter to us if it is through deserts or pleasant fields that we walk, provided God be with us and we be advancing towards heaven." Find the river of calm that flows through the celestial estuaries of the heart, where the Divine Presence conveys an unexplainable presence of a gentle, intimate calmness.

François Fénèlon writes, "The presence of God calms the soul, and gives it quiet and repose." Place the most precious thought on the Beloved, whose peace pervades our longing in subtle and yet hidden visitations, reaching far beyond the wide path of external matter and the brightest of reasoning. St. Gregory the Great writes, "The pursuit of the contemplative life is something for which a great and sustained effort on the part of the powers of the soul is required: an effort to rise from earthly to heavenly things, an effort to keep one's attention fixed on spiritual things, an effort to pass beyond and above the sphere of things visible to the eyes of flesh."

A Return to Love

*It is certain that if God is to be
born in the soul
it must turn back to eternity*

~ *Johannes Tauler*

Trust in Love and don't subscribe to what the world impresses upon your tenderest self, for interior stillness and silent repose are your natural soul state. Open wide the unseen door of your heart's perceptions and allow God to cultivate the Divine love in You. Spirit has been seeking us since the spark of our creation through the celestial lens of love. St. Francis of Assisi reminds us that "what you're looking for is where you're looking from." What I seek, seeks and loves me infinitely more. German mystic Meister Eckhart writes, "The eye with which I see God is the same with which God sees me. My eye and God's eye is one eye and one sight and one knowledge and one love."

Love is the very essence and ground of our being. Love is God's essential nature and the agent for transformative union between creation and Creator. Love alone remains undisturbed by the clamour of surface matter that habitually seeks to cloud the heart with memories captured from a past breeze or fear of future winds. Sufi mystic Kabir writes, "Lift the veil that obscures the heart and there you will find what you are looking for."

Love is revealed interiorly through the fragrant spheres of the soul, where new light is revealed through the sincerity and nakedness of our arrival. As love takes notice of the motion within the heart's intent as Angels gather near, the soul intuitively realises there is nothing more necessary for growth than love itself. As we receive the gift of love, all the barriers we have constructed begin to crack as light penetrates through the old veils. It is important to view our true essence as an essential part of the lattice of love in which we belong and have originated from.

My Hidden Companion

Taste the hidden sweetness that lies within your heart which God has kept for those whose lives are tender within. Place your mind in the softness of life's eternal flow. Place your soul in the brilliance of heaven's endless glow; and love him totally who gave himself for your love, and you will hold him who holds all things in truth.

~ St. Clare of Assisi

Spirit. It is Your hidden essence that I seek from within the rugged landscape of my soul. I feel your vastness compared to this temporal form in which I carry and endlessly labour to. Spirit. You convey your essence from behind the celestial veil, relaying the fragrance of Heaven to my stilled senses, and at times you withdraw yourself from my feelings to test my love for You. But you know my stubbornness to continue through the gift of Your patience in waiting. I always long for your gentle return as I feel you arranging my interior furniture in the twilight beyond my reach, as you create more room for your dwelling within the flowering tabernacle of my soul. By Your grace You have given me the attraction to love Thee, for your hidden touch has left a lasting imprint within this templed vessel as a breath becomes one. Johannes Tauler writes, "Give yourself entirely to God, enter and hide in the hidden ground of your soul." It is here in the depths of soul. Heaven is revealed through an intellectual vision beyond sight, touch, or conceptual thought.

St. John of the Cross writes, "You yourself are the lodging wherein God dwells, and the closet and hiding place wherein He is hidden." How wonderful a life that recognises the beauty of a concealed heaven! The Divine is closer than our most cherished memory, closer than our breath, the Eternal occupier of our heart, whose ascending currents of peace recollect our intention to draw us near. St. Augustine writes, "God who hears you is within you, hidden within, or God who hears you is not merely by your side, and you have no need to go wandering about, no need to be reaching out to God as though you would touch him with your hands." The mystical life teaches us the way to God is uniquely internal. But first, the pilgrim must clear the ground from the personal debris that drowns out the eternal echoes of heaven that emerges unbounded from within our most sacred depth. This unfolding reveals our true nature as the soul in secret communes with the very essence of love. St. Therese of Lisieux writes, "I go to that Divine Furnace to draw out life, And there my Sweet Savior listens to me night and day."

Emanations of a Soul

Paint your house with the colors of modesty and humility. Make it radiant with the light of justice. Decorate it with the finest gold leaf of good deeds. Adorn it with the walls and stones of faith and generosity. Crown it with the pinnacle of prayer. In this way you will make it a perfect dwelling place for the Lord. You will be able to receive him as in a splendid palace, and through his grace you will already possess him, his image enthroned in the temple of your spirit.

~ St. John Chrysostom

Through the medium of reflective silence, we mirror the will of God, widen the lens of clarity, and be drawn by the interior flicker of devotion, whose eternal flame remains undisturbed by the radio of sensory matter. Intuitively, we feel the movement of God by an inward vision that moves without sight or touch, that surcharges the soul by an intellectual light of faith that ignites advancing hearts ever closer towards the inevitable fortress of hidden Love where the language of Divine love is sketched forever upon our hearts. For we are designed by Love, for Love, reflections of light scattered through colourful veils that flicker by the willingness of our sincerity. Marcus Aurelius writes, "The soul becomes dyed with the color of its thoughts." The luminous hues from our devotion magnetically draw God close, for Spirit cannot resist the love that emanates from within a templed heart. Blessed Angela of Foligno writes: "[B]y the virtue of love, is the lover transformed in the beloved and the beloved is transformed in the lover, and like unto hard iron which so assumes the color, heat, virtue, and form of the fire that it almost turns into fire, so does the soul, united with God through the perfect grace of divine love, itself almost become divine and transformed in God." Keep this sacred truth close. Spirit has chosen to dwell in depths of the spiritual heart, for there He waits patiently with mercy upon our inward glance and the openness to receive Her subtle currents of love that melts away all error in God's love. We shall endure as beauty unfolds.

Remain in Me

I who am Divine am truly in you.
I can never be sundered from you:
However far we be parted,
never can we be separated.
I am in you and you are in Me.
We could not be any closer.
We two are fused into one,
poured into a single mould.
Thus, unwearied,
we shall remain
forever.

~ Mechthild of Magdeburg (The Flowing
Light of the Godhead, 13th century)

Raise your sails upon the mighty ocean of life and prepare for all weathers, for the fleeting nature of life can become unruly without much warning during challenging times. Remain rooted within the sanctuary of God's love, for with you, my Lord, we cannot sink below the horizon of your love. St. John Baptist de la Salle writes, "Were you to simply remain in God's presence, that would be a great help to you, supporting you in your troubles and helping you to bear them patiently. Be sure that God is more ready than ever to welcome you into his arms, and that as your distress increases so does his mercy towards you increase and abound."

Despite the fleeting nature of human existence, be humbled in gratitude for Spirit's sublime presence remains unmoved despite the clouds that may gather over the heart's aspirations. God desires us to remain even closer during turbulent times, for Spirit is the celestial breeze that propels us across the vast ocean of life to the infinite shores of permanent peace. St. Teresa of Avila writes, "Let nothing disturb thee, Let nothing dismay thee: All things pass, God never changes. Patience attains All that it strives for. He who has God Finds he lacks nothing: God alone suffice."

Perseverance in Prayer

However we do mental prayer, we can be sure of encountering difficulties. Some have already been mentioned: dryness, distaste, a sense of our own worthlessness, the feeling the effort to pray is useless. The first thing to say about such difficulties is that they should not come as a surprise or cause us to worry or be upset. Not only are they inevitable, they are actually good for us. They purify our love for God and strengthen our faith.

~ Jacques Philippe

Spirit cannot resist our perseverance and continuous willingness to strive in prayer, especially in times of spiritual dryness. St. Julian of Norwich writes, "Pray, even if you feel nothing, see nothing. For even when you are dry, empty, sick or weak, at such a time is your prayer most pleasing to God, although you may find little joy in it." Pray inwardly even though you may not enjoy it, for it does well even when you feel nothing. "Prayer is the deliberate persevering action of the soul. It is true and enduring, and full of grace. Prayer fastens the soul to God and makes it one with his will."

The Divine knows the direction of our hearts in times of felt abandonment when God seems distant. Remember, in such times, deep healing takes place beyond our sensory understanding as our souls become more aligned with its mirrored substance, void of personal interpretation. Spirit heals our deepest wounds far beyond the reach of our mental stamp, for God removes all emotional barriers and obstacles that shadow the little heaven of our soul. Each day, think of the living Spirit and bury your thoughts within the dwelling Presence and allow yourself to be loved and healed within the loving silence of love. St. John of the Cross teaches us to let go in prayer and feel the frenetic concerns of life in the world fall away like the last leaves of Autumn.

Prayer is the key that unlocks and activates the Divine essence to permeate our soul. St. Teresa of Avila was once asked by a religious sister who wanted to know what the saint did in prayer. She replied, "I just allow myself to be loved." Prayer is the only real channel that expands the spiritual heart in which God's Grace may enter into the arteries of our formless heart. Prayer is the intuitive language of the soul, expressing its longing for Spirit. Brother Lawrence, the French Carmelite, reminds us to acquire the daily habit of speaking to God as if we were alone with Him, with familiarity, confidence, and love as to the dearest and most loving of friends. God's greatest desire is to gently lead us deeper into His hallowed space where life blossoms as our souls follow the intuitive calling of love.

Calico Skies

We shall steer safely through every storm so long as our heart is right, our intention fervent, our courage steadfast, and our trust fixed on God.

~ St. Francis de Sales

My Beloved, uplift my soul and take me to rest upon the Divine mantle of Your Sacred Heart, for the struggling Winter has now passed that once rained heavily upon my aspirations. Now I walk forth upon an exiled ground. I pace, filled in gratitude, into your fragrant meadow with a joyous exuberance that transports me closer to the ointment of Your hidden love, a love that soothes my weathered wounds. St. Teresa of Avila writes, "For the storms, like a wave, pass quickly. And the fair weather returns, because the presence of the Lord they experience makes them soon forget everything." Lord upon Your breast, No longer do I feel the tumult roar of surface life, for only You can give me the serenity despite the weather of temporal pressure, of transitory clouds that once shadowed my tenderest self. Divine Pilot, guide me upon these temporal climates that seek to take me away far from Your eternal port. Steady my heart, for no storms shall sweep across the topography of my soul while in the harbour of Your love.

Seeking the Seeker

Teach me to seek You,
for I cannot seek You
unless You teach me,
or find You
unless you show Yourself to me.
Let me seek You in my desire,
Let me desire You in my seeking.
Let me find You by loving you,
Let me love You when I find you.

~ St. Anselm

What I seek also seeks me, and what I pray for also prays for me. I must gather myself up, and there I must dwell in the divine thought of the Beloved. The gift of Spirit's presence reaches out through thinning veils that encase and grace our souls with the glowing rays of celestial gleam. St. Francis of Assisi writes, "The one you are looking for is the One looking."

God seeks us undismayed despite the debris we have placed upon the divine mirror of our hearts that conceal the Divine essence from expressing its heavenly nature. God seeks to bring peace and restfulness to our souls so that the voiceless sermons of love can be received within the openness of intuittive perception. St. Francis de Sales writes: "You know that when the lake is very calm—and when the winds do not agitate its waters—on a very serene night the sky with all its stars is so perfectly reflected in the water that looking down into its depths the beauty of the heavens is as clearly visible as if we were looking up on high. So when our soul is perfectly calm, unstirred and untroubled by the winds of superfluous cares, unevenness of spirit and inconstancy it is very capable of reflecting in itself the image of Our Lord."

Spirit, through our seeking, disband the temporal structures we have blindly created in the forgetfulness of Thee, bestow upon us a clear vision so we can never lose sight of you. Leo Tolstoy writes, "Live seeking God, then you will not live without God." The Divine has interposed a thin veil between our soul, whose heavenly stirring gives expression and the felt experience of a living faith through the medium of our sincerity as we seek the mysterious presence of God's indwelling nature.

E. B. Pusey writes, "In Him we live and move and have our being…

" … since out of Him we could not be, nor exist; we must live, encircled, and enwrapt, and enfolded in and by His Being; we belong to Him, we are encompassed by Him. Every breath we draw is through Him. But more blessedly, we may be in Him by grace. He is the life of our soul, the Being of our being. He wills to knit us to Himself. Not more surely does our blood circulate through our frames, than the life of our souls may flow into us continually from the Spirit of God, never decayed, ever renewed. With Him thou mayest ever be; he will walk with thee by the way; He will talk with thee in thy secret heart; He will be with thee as thy Friend; by night or by day He will not be separated from thee. He will teach thee through all who teach. Through every dispensation of His providence He will instruct thee. He will teach thee to pray by His Spirit within thee. In every trouble He will be with thee, nearer than the trouble, nearest to thy heart, for He will be within thee. He will kindle thee with love, He will strengthen thy faith, He will be Himself thy hope.

"All which He gives thee now shall be the more precious, because they will not be without Himself, but will be tokens of His presence. He will be 'all in all' things to thee now, the very good of all good, the joy of all pleasure, the sweetness of all things sweet, the life of thy life. He will be the essence of all good here, that He may be thine All hereafter, when 'all' will be again 'very good,' because all will be full of Him" (Pusey 1903, 124).

Spirit, you are the wondrous light that ignites my way back to Thee, for your touch upon my soul has fueled my passion to seek You from behind the celestial partition., for my heart intuitively realises that I seek Thee without sight or touch, but through an intellectual vision lamped by the attraction of your tenderest stirring.

Heart Letters

Nothing is sweeter than love; nothing higher, nothing larger, nothing more joyful, nothing fuller, nothing better in heaven or on earth; for love descends from God and, and may not finally rest in anything lower than God.

~ St. Thomas à Kempis

Spirit, transport Your love upon all yearning hearts. Teach us to hear Your voiceless whisper that ascends through the openness of our devotion, connecting us to the invisible life. Lord, remove the temporal encrustations that cloud the spotless light of Your love, for love is our truest nature and celestial birthright and the most fervent joy to embrace our life. St. Augustine writes, "Let us love the light, long to understand it and thirst after if so that led by it we may come to it, and there live for ever."

Love is the guide and polestar of our heart. Love unites us with God, and love is the natural and greatest expression of the unbounded soul.

St. John of the Cross writes, "[T]he more degrees of love the soul has, the more profoundly does it enter into God, and the more is it centered in Him." Lord, direct our steps in the pursuit of love and quench our thirst, for You alone can only satisfy and regenerate the soul. Encircle our hearts with your ethereal warmth so we may become more attentive to Your silent love so that we may gladly advance towards your sacred mystery.

St. Augustine writes, "Love is itself the fulfillment of all our works. There is the goal; that is why we run: we run toward it, and once we reach it, in it we shall find rest." Love is the ordinance of the heart that directs us toward our innate mirrored source. To seek love is to advance in love. Even the thought of love attracts its essence, for we expand by our heart's arduous desire for the Divine love.

The Consolation of Love

Your Love, Lord, How sweet it smells! How good it sounds! How fine it looks! How soft it feels!

~ St. Thomas à Kempis

Beloved, Your gift of Love has touched my soul, giving me the attraction to advance steadily toward Thee. A gentle, intimate stirring, a touch of Your Grace that will never depart from the port of my heart, remains Anchored to You for all Eternity. St. Thomas à Kempis writes, "If I live to be a hundred, I'll still slave for You as though it were the first hour of the first day my heart was warmed by Yours and decided to follow You" (*Consolations* 2017, 240).

My dearest companion, how patient is Your love, even when I travel far in habitual fog, far from the eternal shore. You have remained unconditionally in love with me ever since my very first dawn. You remain the same, lovingly dwelling in this templed frame with Your Angels guarding my advance. Your gift of Presence uplifts my heart to partake in the banquet of Your ineffable love, which is the root and first cause of my Being. We have originated from love, and there we shall return to the beatific vision, to see without veils.

St. Augustine writes, "To fall in love with God is the greatest of all romances; to seek him, the greatest adventure; to find him, the greatest human achievement." The return to love is the very purpose of our existence: to ascend to that in which we have our very being. Love enters into its very composition and looks forward to a communion of good as its very end goal. St. Bernard of Clairvaux writes, "We are to love God for Himself, because of a twofold reason; nothing is more reasonable, nothing more profitable. Of all the movements, sensations and feelings of the soul, love is the only one in which the creature can respond to the Creator and make some sort of similar return however unequal though it be."

The spiritual life is a return to love, a life free from the egoic stamp of personal ideals and concepts. Brave is the soul that steps out beyond the horizon of the limiting self, entering through the borderless gate that leads to the narrow path of infinite love. St. Thomas à Kempis writes, "Love flies, runs, leaps for joy; it is free and unrestrained. Love gives all for all, resting in One who is highest above all things, from whom every good flows and proceeds. Love does not regard the gifts, but turns to the Giver of all good gifts. Love knows no limits, but ardently transcends all bounds. Love feels no burden, takes no account of toil, attempts things beyond its strength; love sees nothing as impossible, for it feels able to achieve all things. Love therefore does great things; it is strange and effective; while he who lacks love faints and fails." Love is the polyester and very ground of our being. The seeking soul recognises its reflective nature by the consolation of intuitive knowledge. That subtlety arrives unexpectedly and unrecognised by the intellect or sensory reasoning, despite all its mindful discourse. For God cannot be felt or known by the intellect. Our hearts are naturally drawn to love. To imitate love is to advance in love. Thomas Merton writes, "Love is not just a sentiment. Love is being itself. It's like a spring coming up out of the ground of our own depths" (*The Springs of Contemplation* 1992, 16).

Renewed by Change

We become what we love and who we love shapes what we become. If we love things, we become a thing. If we love nothing, we become nothing. Imitation is not a literal mimicking of Christ, rather it means becoming the image of the beloved, an image disclosed through transformation. This means we are to become vessels of God's compassionate love for others.

~ St. Clare of Assisi

God's transformative mystery directs and reclaims our hearts from the burdens of the egoic self that serves only to distance the soul from its spiritual inheritance. As seekers of love, we must be bravely willing to lose parts of our old selves that no longer serve our soul's higher purpose. Never fear change, for a life is not lived if you remain in habitual stagnation. Step out beyond the range of comfort, for nothing is gained by ease alone. St. Joan of Arc inspires us to "Go forward bravely. Fear nothing.

Trust in God; all will be well." Through the mystery of grace, Spirit shapes our hearts in secret behind the scenes of our life, giving us the subtle attraction to enter therein to partake in the Divine mystery. And the paradox is, we will always remain our authentic self. Only the debris that surrounds our soul is dissolved by the current of love that uplifts us upon a higher ground.

T. T. Carter writes, "It is not that we lose anything of our own true nature through this mysterious transformation, we are still our own true selves. Our individuality and special characteristics of being remain. All that is truly ours only becomes more intensely ours, for our true nature becomes more real. The only change is that our nature is pervaded by a life and love beyond it, transforming it into a divine order ever more and more perfectly. And as our efforts prevail to preserve a life of stillness and repose, of faith and love, of prayer and watchfulness, and a pure intention, this diviner life in us is increasingly strengthened and enlarged. All is transformed and raised as more and more we unite ourselves with the amazing mystery of the Presence which is in-habiting our being, working out Its purposes in us, and which is already ours in Its immeasurable and inexhaustible depth of love" (Carter 1903, 125.)

The Fragrance of Prayer

Prayer is the light of the spirit, true knowledge of God, mediating between God and man. The spirit, raised up to heaven by prayer, clings to God with the utmost tenderness; like a child crying tearfully for its mother, it craves the milk that God provides. It seeks the satisfaction of its own desires, and receives gifts outweighing the whole world of nature. Prayer stands before God as an honoured ambassador. It gives joy to the spirit, peace to the heart. I speak of prayer, not words. It is the longing for God, love too deep for words, a gift not given by man but by God's grace.

~ St. John Chrysostom

Along the narrow way, we must fill our hearts with genuine humility and avoid anything that may displease the indwelling Host from conveying Heaven to our souls. God can't resist revealing His essence in response to a sincere prayer that ascends from the very depths of our Being. St. Pio writes, "Prayer is the best weapon we possess. It is the key that opens the heart of God." The quintessence of prayer is the upliftment of the heart to God. St. John Paul writes, "Prayer can truly change your life. For it turns your attention away from yourself and directs your mind and your heart toward the Lord." Prayer is an inexhaustible treasure that brings much spiritual abundance. A prayer that originates from the heart brings a hidden warmth of celestial love to the soul. God seeks our sincerity and the nakedness of our arrival in prayer.

As we gaze upon Eternity, although obscured in vision, we arrive incomplete but full of gratitude for God's unseen touch that connects us to the invisible life. Blessed Charles De Foucauld writes, "Prayer is just conversation with God: listening to him; speaking with him; gazing upon him in silence. The best prayer is the one in which there is the most love. Adoration, wordless admiration, that is the most eloquent form of prayer: that wordless admiration which contains the most passionate declaration of love."

Spirit conveys His essence to a prayerful soul whom by Grace recollects its transitory senses as the intuittive faculties take precedence over the egoic false self. Our soul dwells in two worlds, a world of sense as well as the world of Spirit, which goes unseen to the senses but yet is very much present, especially in times of silent prayer. Thomas Merton writes, "In prayer we discover what we already have. You start from where you are and you deepen what you already have, and you realize you are already there. We have everything but we don't know it and don't experience it. Everything has been given us in Christ. All we need is to experience what we already possess."

In prayer we rediscover our true nature. We are not gaining a new dispensation, but regaining the treasure that is already buried but yet ever present and available under the debris of forgetfulness of who we are. St. Jane Frances de Chantal teaches us that prayer is believing that God is more in us than we are in ourselves. The soul by nature is focused on God's hidden operations and seeks to be trans-formed into the Divine likeness. Prayer unites the soul to God and their Spirit transmits a joy unutterable.

St. Paul of the Cross writes, "Sometimes, in prayer, God communicates to the soul, all at once, His treasures of lights and heavenly graces. Imagine that you have in your hand a golden dish, that you pour into it the extract of the rarest and most exquisite perfumes, and that you steep into it a fine cambric handkerchief; this handkerchief will yield a delicious and inexplicable odor composed of all the perfumes. It is thus my soul feels when I receive those intimate and hidden communications."

The Advancement of Light

Let us love the light, long to understand it and thirst after if so that led by it we may come to it, and there live forever.

~ St. Augustine

Spirit, You lamp all hearts with Your splendorous light, the living flame that guides and ignites our way back home to the divine mantle of Your blessedness. May the gleam of Your infinite light saturate our souls on even our most wearisome day, when the consolation of Your peace hides amongst the clouds. But yet You remain with us undisturbed by fleeting matters of surface life. Meister Eckhart writes, "The Divine Light permeates the soul, and lifts it above the turmoil of temporal things to rest in God. The soul cannot progress except with the light which God has given it as a nuptial gift; love works the likeness of God into the soul." Lord, your dwelling light remains hidden, dimmed by the world's directionless scramble that seems to rush against an endless current of restlessness. Your luminous light resides beyond the horizon of gain and self-interest. Soul, You are a spark of Infinite Light, templed in form, wrapped in layers, a living reflection of mirrored beauty and felt mystery. You travel alone upon an invisible path, enshrined by a love unseen, lamped by the interior light of Heaven that enkindles our hearts within the Divine glow of reflective love.

Dante writes, "The love of God, unutterable and perfect, flows into a pure soul the way light rushes into a transparent object. The more love that it finds, the more it gives itself: so that as we grow clear and open, the more complete the joy of heaven is." Allow God's love to surge through the open manifolds of the surrendering heart, for anything that is not in balance with the celestial light will be whisked away by transformative waves of Divine love that in time will envelop each aspect of our Being through the intent of our continuous willingness to advance in the light of love. St. John of Avila writes, "Retire into the secrecy of your own heart and open it to receive what is wont to come from so powerful a Light. Beseech the same Lord that, as He has deigned to place Himself within your hands, He will give you the further grace to esteem and venerate and love Him as you should."

Go Beyond in Silence

How fleeting all earthly things are, and everything that appears great disappears like smoke, and does not give the soul freedom, but weariness. Happy the soul that understands these things and with only one foot touches the earth.

~ St. Faustina

Set your heart upon the Beloved and turn your inward gaze far beyond the mental advertisers and the fleeting traffic of life that grasp to purchase your precious time. Remain steadfast in love upon the unruly waves of life and prepare your heart for all seasons. For a life that seeks ease is a life yet to be lived. St. Francis de Sales writes, "Steer safely through every storm, so long as our heart is right, our intention fervent, our courage steadfast, and our trust fixed on God. Keep your toes unbounded from the weight of anchoring grounds. The mind by nature is cautious with its transport to change or challenge." St. Catherine of Siena reminds us of the powerlessness of the mind whenever the celestial breeze sweeps over our soul. She writes, "For what is the mind to do with something that becomes the mind's ruin: a God that consumes us in His grace." By the gift of grace there is so much to discover, more space to recover, for the mind in its fullness cannot produce such a Divine gesture. Under the guise of self we are powerless, and without direction in Spirit we dissolve steadily. All that clouds the aspirations of the heart. What isn't aligned for the betterment of the soul will be consumed by grace. St. Thomas à Kempis writes: "So also the more perfectly a man renounces things of this world, and the more completely he dies to himself through contempt of self, the more quickly this great grace comes to him, the more plentifully it enters in, and the higher it uplifts the free heart."

A Divine Gesture

Leave to God, when it comes, the length and manner of the heavenly visitation.

~ St. Thomas à Kempis

In silence, slip away from the endless commentaries and the colourless rush of traffic that absorb so much precious time. Enter the gentleness of breath where nothing lacks within the iridescence of solitude. The soul roams, hidden from sight, along paths lamped by an untouched vision. God's gift of grace leads us through the vast desert of our hearts, drawing us close to His sacred Presence and trust in the Divine counsel that ascends its unique dialect to our intellectual hearts. Blessed Fulton Sheen writes, "[Y]ou give me your humanity, and I will give you my Divinity; you give me your time, and I will give you My eternity; you give me your broken heart, and I will give you Love; you give me your nothingness, and I will give you My all."

My Beloved, I wander through your vast spheres, seeking you. Then, unknowingly, the gift of your peace captures my heart, suspending all striving, freeing me momentarily from the constraints of time and narrative of mind. There remains something unexplainable that the mind cannot reach. Despite all its transport, it won't produce the subtle currents of inner peace that ascends its sweet aroma through the open manifolds that take us from pain to peace, from struggle to contentment. Meister Eckhart reminds us that there is a place in the soul where we can never be wounded. In this divine centre, no earthly thing can consume the eternal light that dwells in our deepest self, where Spirit imparts a little bouquet of Heaven. God cannot resist the perseverance and readiness of a seeking heart to receive.

Meister Eckhart writes, "Be prepared at all times for the gifts of God and be ready always for new ones. For God is a thousand times more ready to give than we are to receive." Spirit dwells far beyond all personal self-knowing and mental concepts, for the individual mind, with all its ingenuity, cannot re-enact such a divine gesture. Entwine your sincerity for union within these blessed visitations, no matter how fleeting as the alluring peace of Spirit draws you forth through dissolving debris that no longer can claim you for its own.

A Love Unknown

Live in the joy and the peace of the divine Majesty. Live lost in divine love. Live for divine love and of divine love.

~ St. Paul of the Cross

The Divine is omnipresent and reflected throughout all creation, present within the aspirations of all desiring hearts. God's indwelling Presence is present within each created soul. When we become aware of this Divine truth, we recognize and experience an unfolding of hearts in the Great Divine Romance. French Carmelite St. Elizabeth of the Trinity writes, "We carry our heaven within us, since He who completely satisfies every longing of the glorified souls in the light of the Beatific Vision, is giving Himself to us in faith and mystery. It is the same thing. It seems to me I have found my heaven on earth, since heaven is God and God is in my soul. The day I understood that, everything became clear to me and I wish I could whisper this secret to those

I love in order that they also might cling closely to God through everything."

Our true purpose and mission in life is to cleave towards the abiding presence of Love, for there is nothing on this Earth that can match the celestial Love that stirs gracefully between an individual soul and the indwelling Spirit. Where your Presence is my Lord, there is my joy, my humility, and my living fortress from the clouds that seek to claim and consume me for their own. Love is my being, and my soul aspires to return to that in which it has its very Being. Lord, you are the flowering radiance of all sincere hearts, whose fragrance permeates a purity of Love that is intimately gentle, uncomplicated, translucent, and satisfying to the soul.

St. Elizabeth of the Trinity writes, "My God, What a joyous mystery is Your presence within me, in that intimate sanctuary of my soul where I can always find You." The presence of God permeates and is reflected through the sincerity and interior longings of a devoted heart that reflects outward from the gentleness of our movements. Allow this heavenly truth to sweep over your soul. St. Julian of Norwich reminds us to "Live gladly because of the knowledge of his Love." A Love that is embracing, delightful, and ever present, ever anew, even when we may feel distant from the Divine Presence. Remember that the essence of our being is Love.

From Love we came, in Love we move, and to Love we shall return.

St. Thomas à Kempis writes, "Nothing is sweeter than love, nothing more courageous, nothing higher, nothing wider, nothing more pleasant, nothing fuller nor better in Heaven and Earth: because Love is born of God, and cannot rest but in God" (à Kempis 2004, 114). The surrender to God's presence is a trusted martyrdom of the heart, whether in times of visiting consolations or through trials for God's Love for us is unchangeable through the unpredictable seasons of life. Trust in God that despite the debris that congests the gentle arteries of the spiritual heart, the soul's only true desire is to find repose in the Divine sanctuary of the immeasurable Love, despite the clamouring, vain noise that bellows around its ascending inspirations for union.

François Fénèlon writes, "God never ceases to speak to us, but the noise of the world without and the tumult of our passions within bewilder us and prevent us from listening to Him." Encircle the ardour of your heart with thoughts of Love. Make of your devotion a nest of love fit for your Heavenly Host to dwell and come drink from the wellspring of your devotion as our hearts yearn to dwell with the multitude of Love.

The Topography of a Veiled Heart

There exists in our heart an interior land where we are alone, to which no one finds his way but God. This innermost, unfrequented chamber of our heart is really there—the only question is whether we ourselves avoid it foolishly… because no one and no familiar things of this earth can accompany us if we enter it.

~ Karl Rahner

The spiritual heart is a formless organ of perception and the gateway whereupon Grace enters and flows through its open manifolds. Spirit. Through the abyss of your Eternity, you sketch your heavenly ordinances upon all seeking hearts, transmitting your odorous essence of abiding Presence to our recollected senses. God's essence exalts the heart with what is initially felt as peace, joy, and an unexplainable love that the intellect cannot reach or find reason upon their arrival. St. Thomas à Kempis writes: "Christ will come to you offering His consolation, if you prepare a fit dwelling for Him in your heart, whose beauty and glory, wherein He takes delight, are all from within. His visits with the inward man are frequent, His communion sweet and full of consolation, His peace great, and His intimacy wonderful indeed. Therefore, faithful soul, prepare your heart for this Bridegroom that He may come and dwell within you."

When we feel an unexplainable beauty, it is God's movement swelling within a joyous heart. Mother Teresa said that a joyful heart is the inevitable result of a heart burning with love. Make of your heart a fit dwelling place for your heavenly Host, whose peace counsels and gives repose to all seeking hearts and who tends to our greatest needs. St. Thérèse writes: "Let us make a little tabernacle in our heart where Jesus may take refuge, and then He will be consoled and He will forget what we cannot forget."

The Place of Refuge

Let us take refuge from this world. You can do this in spirit, even if you are kept here in the body. You can at the same time be here and present to the Lord. Your soul must hold fast to him, you must follow after him in your thoughts, and you must tread his ways by faith, not in outward show. You must take refuge in him. He is your refuge and your strength.

~ St. Ambrose of Milan

Through clouds of struggle and trial, it is important to leave a piece of your heart in the illumined light of the Spirit. Despite the unpredictability of life, keep the prayerful thought of Heaven close in your heart. God desires us to come close to His healing salve, especially in times of adversity. St. John Chrysostom writes, "Prayer is the place of refuge for every worry, a foundation for cheerfulness, a source of constant happiness, a protection against sadness." The heart is the mirrored reflection of resilience and yet gently selfless by nature. Lord, You are the hidden fortitude that beckons us to take shelter from the harsh rains that wound our tenderest self, calling us in from the storm that howls against our better nature. St. Teresa of Avila writes, "For the storms, like a wave, pass quickly. And the fair weather returns, because the presence of the Lord they experience makes them soon forget everything." Spirit in the fortress of your Divine heart, all feelings of anxiety are dispersed by your intimate breeze.

Thomas à Kempis writes, "When the grace of God comes to us we can do all things, but when it leaves us, we become poor and weak, abandoned as it were, to affliction. Yet, in this condition we should not become dejected or despair. On the contrary, we should calmly await the will of God and bear whatever befalls us in praise of Jesus Christ; for after winter comes the summer, after night comes the day, and after the storm, a great calm." Spirit seeks to impress upon us the intuitive understanding that in the shelter of our formless heart emanates a reflective, healing love, a place of sanctuary where Angels dwell.

St. Padre Pio compares the fortress of the heart to that of the Kingfisher who builds their nest by the sea. They build it in a tightly compressed, circular form so that the seawater cannot penetrate it. Here these little birds place their young ones so when the sea comes upon them by surprise, they can swim with confidence and float on the waves. The saint continues, I want your heart to be like this, well compact and closed on all sides so if the worries and storms of the world come upon it, it will not be penetrated. Leave but one opening to your heart that is towards heaven. Beloved, may Your heavenly rays of healing light saturate our hearts and place us upon higher grounds. Preserve your peace within our glancing hearts, and may your voiceless counsel tend to our greatest needs.

Life's Pendulum

Let not your faith and love be weakened by your pain and trouble. A large fire is increased, rather than quenched by the wind; so, though a weak love of God is, like a candle, easily extinguished by the first puff of air, yet true charity gains force and courage by its trials. This is the fire which comes down from heaven which no water of tribulation can extinguish. I pray God may open your eyes and let you see what hidden treasures he bestows on us in the trials from which the world thinks only to flee. Shame turns into honor when we seek God's glory. Present affliction becomes the source of heavenly glory.

~ St. John of Avila

Hidden under the surface currents of life, the soul roams upon its unique path, concealed from sensory traffic and intellectual reasoning. Our spirit by nature is not destined for the grave of a wintered life, yet we must travel along mountainous terrains. God has placed many portals along the weathered lanes of a silent land. The wise heart intuitively understands that life is like a pendulum that swings between both trial and consolation, but God is equally experienced in both shadow and light.

Blessed John Henry Newman writes, "You must make up your mind to the prospect of sustaining a certain measure of pain and trouble in your passage through life." The soul cannot expand its scope by the seeking comfort of mindful ease or relaxed pleasure. St. Augustine writes, "Even here, amidst trials and temptations let us, let all men, sing alleluia. God is faithful, says Holy Scripture, and He will not allow you to be tried beyond your strength. So let us sing alleluia, even here on earth. Man is still a debtor, but God is faithful. Scripture does not say that he will not allow you to be tried, but that he will not allow you to be tried beyond your strength. Whatever the trial, he will see you through it safely, and so enable you to endure. You have entered upon a time of trial but you will come to no harm—God's help will bring you through it safely. You are like a piece of pottery shaped by instruction, fired by tribulation. When you are put into the oven therefore, keep your thoughts on the time when you will be taken out again; for God is faithful, and he will guard both your going in and your coming out."

Despite the cold that presses against the heart's aspirations, keep one toe above the weight of anchoring trials. The soul has its seasons, but underneath turbulent winds, the fragrance of spring blooms within the shadow and light of the celestial dew. God leads the soul back home in numerous ways, at times to test our love and strength to persevere therein through the interior map to His Divine dwelling.

St. Pio writes, "Why should you worry whether God wants you to reach the heavenly home by way of the desert or by the fields, when by the one as well as by the other one arrives all the same at a Blessed Eternity? Keep far from you excessive preoccupation which arises from the trials which the good God wishes to visit upon you." Remain steadfast upon life's unruly waves. Find repose in moments of visiting trial and rest lovingly in the thought of God, who desires only the best for the soul's development. St. Francis de Sales writes, "Do not give into fear in the face of the changes and chances of this life. Rather, as they arise, look at them with full trust in God, to whom you belong, who will enable you—through His powerful love— to profit from them. He has guided you thus far in life; so hold fast to His dear hand, and He will lead you safely through every trial. Whenever you cannot stand, He will carry you in His loving arms."

The Interior Battlefield

To remain stationary for a long time is impossible. The man who makes no gain loses the little he has gained. The man who does not climb upward goes down the ladder. The man who does not vanquish is himself vanquished. Our life is lived amid perilous battles. If we do not fight we perish, but we cannot resist without winning, nor can we win without a victory.

~ St. Francis de Sales

Brave is the soul who carries their opened heart along the rugged battlefield of life, for the greatest battles take place behind closed eyes and are the ones fought and won within the vast topography of the soul. For the most wounded of souls who have persevered along the path of return carry the most hidden scars, yet their eyes reflect an imprinted serenity established by love. God will only give us trials in the form of subtle lessons that the world seems to normally flee from or subconsciously bury within the emotional debris, only to blanket the soul further from expressing its true expressive purpose. St. Maximilian Kolbe writes, "The real conflict is inner conflict. … And what use are victories on the battlefield if we ourselves are defeated in our innermost personal selves?" It takes special bravery to sail beyond the horizon of self struggles in the hidden pursuit of love.

On spiritual combat, Pope John Paul II writes, "It is a secret and interior art, an invisible struggle." It is the little unseen victories that bring an ardour to our hearts to preserve therein despite the interior weather. St. Faustina in her diary entry of 1760 writes: "Always fight with the deep conviction that I am with you. Do not be guided by feeling, because it is not always under your control. but all merit lies in the will. I will not delude you with prospects of peace and consolations. On the contrary, prepare for great battles. Know that you are now on a great stage where all heaven and earth are watching you. Fight like a knight so that I can reward you. Do not be unduly fearful because you are not alone."

St. Henry Suso says: "Remember that you will derive strength by reflecting that the saints yearn for you to join their ranks; desire to see you fight bravely, and that you behave like true knights in your encounters with the same adversities which they had to conquer, and that breathtaking joy is theirs and your eternal reward for having endured a few years of temporal pain. Every drop of earthly bitterness will be changed into an ocean of heavenly sweetness." Despite the weight of life that presses against the heart's aspirations, keep the thought of God cradled in your heart. Like nature, the soul has its seasons, but underneath turbulent weather, the fragrance of spring blooms within the dance of shadow and light. C. S. Lewis writes, "God allows us to experience the low points of life in order to teach us lessons that we could learn in no other way."

A Living Faith

Faith is our light in this life. By it we know the truth without seeing it, we are put in touch with what we cannot feel, recognize what we cannot see, and view the world stripped of all its outer shell. Faith unlocks God's treasury. It is the key to all the vastness of His wisdom. The emptiness of all created things is disclosed by faith, and it is by faith that God reveals Himself.

~ Jean-Pierre de Caussade

Spirit, fill the cup of our soul with Your mystical presence. Melt our hearts within the living flame of Your merciful love. Pierce through the midst of all mindful reasoning, recollect our senses and lead us to the interior mirror of Your beauty. As we gaze upon Thee, may our eyes reflect an imprint of Your serenity.

St. Gregory of Nyssa writes, "Faith is the womb that conceives this new life." Beloved by the gift of grace, your dwelling is revealed beyond the security of a mere belief that's mentally locked within its clouded border. The ancient pilgrimage teaches that the mind first must become subservient to the heart. St. Madeline Sophie Barat writes, "Let your heart be more attentive than your head, for the Holy Spirit is love, and to take hold, it is more important to love than to understand." Faith is an experience that the mind cannot produce despite its thinking talents.

St. Augustine writes, "Faith is to believe what you do not see. The reward of faith is to see what you believe." Blessed is the soul who feels without touch, sees a vision beyond sensory sight to experience void of an understanding. For God's essence is the veiled paradise and the unseen mystery that ascends through the mirrored reflection of our intuitive hearts, where Spirit conveys secretly His voiceless sermons in subtle waves hidden from mindful interpretation, linked by golden threads that transmit Heaven upon us.

God cannot be conceptualised by thought or engineered by mere belief, for these are secondary means. Faith is a felt experience, a Grace that reveals the hidden Eternal. Thomas Merton reminds us that faith is the beginning of a new life, for what no longer serves the soul's deepest desire will be dissolved by the luminous light of faith.

A Thoughtless Prayer

When your mind does wander during prayer, bring it back. When it wanders again, bring it back again. Each and every time that you read a prayer while your thoughts are wandering (and consequently you read it without attention and feeling,) then do not fail to read it again. Even if your mind wanders several times in the same place, read it again and again until you read it all the way through with understanding and feeling. In this way, you will overcome this difficulty so that the next time, perhaps, it will not come up again, or if it does return, it will be weaker.

~ St. Theophan the Recluse

We cannot be defined by the narrative of thought. Even in prayer, our sincerity can't be diluted by passing clouds unless we give permission to follow. Do not cling to that which is not your nature. Referring to thoughts, St. Clement Hofbauer writes, "[W]e should think of them as little as we do of the leaves that fall down from trees." Saintly souls shared in different forms the same struggles as we do, but they were content in their Being and accepted the path that God had chosen for them, whether it be through consolation or trial. St. Francis de Sales encourages us in the following: "Be who you are and be that well. So that you may bring honour to the Master Craftsman whose handiwork you are."

We can be at times quite critical of our spiritual progress. This too is a distraction. Acceptance and compassion of ourselves is key to arrive in prayer as we are. We are not our thoughts nor can we be defined by them. Despite the distractions we may feel in prayer, take confidence that we are the mirrored reflection of an all-consuming love that pervades each open manifold of our hearts. Jacques Philippe writes, "Distractions are one of the more common difficulties in prayer. They are absolutely normal and should neither surprise nor sadden us. When we realize that we have become distracted from our prayer and our thoughts are wandering, rather than getting discouraged or angry, we should simply, peacefully and gently bring our minds back to God." Be gentle with yourself. If you feel that you have drifted, of course, simply return your inner gaze back to the original intent: to commune and convey your heart with God in silence.

François Fénèlon reminds us to listen rather less to our own thoughts so as to be able to listen more to

God. The Beloved can't convey His contemplative essence to a busy mind that drifts outward by the swell of mental commentaries. Raïssa Maritain writes, "Contemplation is a silent prayer which takes place in recollection in the secret of the heart and is directly ordered to union with God." The Divine reveals His essence through the sincerity of a silent heart recollected, resting upon its source.

St. John Climacus writes, "The lover of silence draws closer to God." In voiceless prayer it is only God that can hear your soul's voice as the tumult of the world seems but a distant memory suspended in time as the Divine visitation ignites our intuitive faculties free from the entanglement of thought. St. Thomas Aquinas writes, "A heart which is free from thoughts and affections alien to God is like a temple consecrated to the Lord, in which we can contem-plate him even in this world." St. Teresa of Avila advises us not to let ourselves be frightened by our own thoughts. Accept that thoughts may arise in prayer, but do not cling to their roots. Acknowledge them, remaining unattached, and like clouds they shall pass, and by grace, clarity of intent to be with God in prayer will return. Francisco de Osuna writes, "This is the highest effect left by grace received by this means in the soul, from which it casts out all superfluous cares and idle thoughts which distract men and drive them outside themselves."

A Personal Cross

I know what sort of a being I am; yet even though I feel myself miserable, I am not troubled at it; nay, I am sometimes joyful at it, considering that I am a truly fit object for the mercy of God, to which I continually recommend you.

~ St. Francis de Sales

For the soul to remain close to God, it must be aware and have an intuitive understanding of its internal pains. This awareness that the multitudes seem willing to flee from introduces daring hearts to the celestial balm of the Divine Physician. No one is immune to suffering upon these temporal grounds. Keep on keeping on, humming to the beat of eternal hope that has been placed in your most sacred Self. St. Augustine writes, "Whatever the trial, he will see you through it safely, and so enable you to endure. You have entered upon a time of trial, but you will come to no harm. God's help will bring you through it safely. You are like a piece of pottery, shaped by instruction, fired by tribulation. When you are put into the oven therefore, keep your thoughts on the time when you will be taken out again; for God is faithful, and he will guard both your going in and your coming out."

Heaven is close in time of tribulations, for such pains guide us towards the humility of heart. St. Francis de Sales writes, "When we happen to fall, let us cast down our heart before God." The Divine is our refuge and elixir of the soul who transfigures and molds our brokenness by visitations of new light. Make of your heart a fortress, a sanctuary of calmness, a place of return upon the whim of a steady breath that enters the innermost chamber where Spirit conveys Her essence to our weary hearts.

St. Ambrose of Milan writes, "You must take refuge in Him. He is your refuge and your strength." Dwelling with God and surrendering our Will to the Divine Will during adversities bring the soul great merit and healing. The multitude seeks a life of avoidance through chasing comfort, living a preoccupied existence, unaware of the true beauty of life with its infinite attributes when anchored with God, who draws our love through the transports of adversity, where the soul gains little victories over its egoic struggles. St. Francis de Sales reminds us that the actions we perform in dryness are more meritorious in the sight of God than those which we perform in consolation. God would only send us adversity to draw from it His own glory and our salvation. Let us think well on this truth, and regard only God in all events, and all events only in God. St. Francis continues: "If any accident surprises our heart immediately, it has recourse to the Divinity, acknowledging that when the world looks dark or alone is good, and when danger threatens it, alone is good; and when danger threatens, it, alone can save and preserve."

The Way of Humility

Humility, that is lowliness or self-abasement, is an inward bowing down or prostrating of the heart and of the conscience before God's transcendent worth… For to pay homage to God by every outward and inward act, this is the first and dearest work of humility, the most savory among those of charity, and most meet among those of righteousness.

~ Blessed John Ruysbroeck

Humility is the true foundation of spiritual life, the more we descend into our depths it seems a wider vision comes into view, as the hidden way begins to appear beyond the horizon of self-interest and intellectual reasoning with all its colourful transports. Gabriel of St. Mary Magdalen writes, "The deeper, and firmer it is, the better the house will be and the greater assurance of stability it will have… Humility is the firm bedrock upon which every Christian should build the edifice of his spiritual life….Humility forms the foundation of charity by emptying the soul of pride, arrogance, disordered love of self and of one's own excellence, and by replacing them with the love of God and our neighbour." Humility holds more purpose than a cup that overflows with stamped honours of mental accomplishments.

St. Giles of Assisi writes, "No man can attain the knowledge of God but by humility." If we desire to dwell with the Divine, we must step away from all knowing and in secret, turn our grace-filled gaze away from the habitual clouds that cast temporal shadows over our souls' greatest aspirations. It takes a special gift of courage to step beyond any impressions of self-importance. Paradoxically, to lose yourself is to gain eternal joys. St. John Vianney writes, "Humility is like a pair of scales: the lower one side falls, the higher rises the other." Humility is not a weakness. Thomas Merton reminds us that humility is the surest sign of strength. Acts through a humbled heart, open to grace but void of self gain, yet aware of its incompleteness. The soul roams, strengthened by the attraction of love. Humility transforms our heart by enabling us to feel our own incompleteness and that of others, giving rise to an expansive feeling of compassion. St. Francis de Sales writes, "Humility makes our heart meek towards the perfect and the imperfect towards the former through reverence towards the latter through compassion." The ambient essence of humility truly encompasses our hearts. It not only creates a solid foundation for a spiritual life, but its nutrients also enrich the soul by attracting celestial light that pierces through the self-constructed veils where little victories appear as interior felt transitions.

Francisco de Osuna writes, "The soul is like wax that, placed in the sunlight, melts for love of the ray that His Majesty infuses in it. Humility gives the soul strength to persevere, making known to it that as wax hardens when removed from the sunlight, so the soul, turning from God, will become hard again and lose the recollection and tender love it received from the Lord." Humility nourishes our interior garden. Its sunlit dew casts no shadow over the flowering aspirations of the soul who seeks its source just as a flower ascends towards the first particles of morning light, whose fragrant, sweet-smelling oils emit an electric field, enticing nature to come close.

St. Anthony of Padua writes, "The spirit of humility is sweeter than honey, and those who nourish themselves with this honey produce sweet fruit. "Be rooted in humanity. Never fear that we will lose ourselves. We only polish the mirror of our hearts to gain a better version, and yet our uniqueness remains individually woven in the Divine mystery. St. Paul of the Cross writes, "[G]round yourself in true humility and know your nothingness. A time will come when the Holy Spirit will blow upon the ashes, and a fire more lively and bright that before will be lit because you have been faithful to God."

A Brighter Courage

To have courage for whatever comes in life—everything lies in that.

~ St. Teresa of Avila

Beloved, despite the weather that obscures the vision, may our hearts remain swollen with courage within your perpetual brightness. St. Francis de Sales writes, "Even though everything turns and changes around us, we must always remain unchanging and ever looking, striving, and aspiring toward God" (de Sales 1972, 243). Upon life's unruly ter-rain, step forth courageously, for we are the mir-rored reflections of an all-consuming love that pervades our souls. Allow this truth to settle deep within you. Never feel disheartened, for God will never abandon you, but will always encourage you to draw closer to Her infinite heart.

St. Padre Pio of Pietrelcina writes, "Do not be discouraged, because, if there is a continuous effort to improve in the soul, in the end the Lord rewards it by making it suddenly blossom in all its virtues as in a flower garden." Don't get caught up in feelings of imperfections, for they only block the celestial gleam that illuminates the soul from expressing its intrinsic nature. See that your love for God is sincere and never feel discouraged despite feelings of incompleteness. St. Elizabeth of the Trinity writes, "One must erase the word discouragement from one's dictionary of love." Move courageously, for life isn't designed for ease and comfort. It is only through its diverse seasons that the seeds of love are nurtured. Despite the turbulent winds that seek to distract the heart from its formless course in surrendering faith, remain unanchored from the weight of its mental narratives. Give all to God.

St. Francis de Sales writes, "Go courageously to do whatever you are called to do. If you have any fears, say to your soul: The Lord will provide for us." If your weakness troubles you, cast yourselves on God and trust in Him. The apostles were mostly unlearned fishermen, but God gave them learning enough for the work they had to do. Trust in Him, depend on His providence. Fear nothing. It is necessary that we endeavour to preserve a constant and inviolable equality of the heart amidst so great an inequality of events. Although all things turn and change around us, we must always remain unchanging, ever looking, striving, and aspiring toward our God.

François Fénelon writes, "Never let us be discouraged with ourselves; it is not when we are conscious of our faults that we are the most wicked: on the contrary, we are less so. We see by a brighter light. And let us remember, for our consolation, that we never perceive our sins till He begin to cure them." Our soul, intuitively by nature understands that experiencing a human existence is vital for its evolution. It is aware a life to be lived cannot be void of suffering. St. John of the Cross reminds us that suffering brings with it the purest and most intimate knowledge of God, and consequently the purest and highest joy. Fellow Carmelite St. Therese of Lisieux writes, "He longs to give us a magnificent reward. He knows that suffering is the only means of preparing us to know Him as He knows Himself, and to become ourselves divine." On our journey back home to the Divine, may we never hold onto feelings of discouragement, but find a new strength by abandoning ourselves upon the sacred mantle of Her infinite peace.

An Ever-New Love

Love is itself the fulfillment of all our works. There is the goal; that is why we run: we run toward it, and once we reach it, in it we shall find rest.

~ St. Augustine

Love is the very ground and light of our being. From the love we came, in Love we move, and to love we shall return. Francisco de Osuna writes, "Let us find ourselves… in love, root ourselves in it like trees, build ourselves on it as a firm foundation founded on love for God which makes us his mansion and his temple in which he dwells; let us, rooted in love." There is nothing more delightful than a soul that emanates a love void of the entanglement of personal complexities, a love that transcends constraints that press upon a soul's better nature.

St. Thomas à Kempis writes, "Love is a great thing, yea, a great and thorough Good; by itself it makes everything that is heavy, light … and makes everything that is bitter, sweet and tasteful" (*Imitation*, 114).

St. Therese reminds us that love is all things; love is eternal. An ancient love that shimmers throughout the generations of the rare noble-hearted, the uplifters. Love unifies the soul to Spirit. Love itself brings a form of intuitive knowing, a felt vision beyond the ordinary sensory field. Meister Eckhart taught that "God's ground and the soul's ground is one ground." It is the Unitive life of Divine Love. St. Catherine of Genoa writes, "Love has been the beginning and the middle of thy course. it must also be the end. Thou canst not live without it: it is thy life in this world and the next, for it is I."

Love is honey to the soul, a sweet nectar, an ethereal balm, a delight that transcends all constraints that weigh against its aspirations. For love alone makes the soul return to the true repose of its natural state, void of the egoic entanglement of complexities. St. John of the Cross writes, "Love unites the soul with God, and, the more degrees of love the soul has, the more profoundly does it enter into God and the more is it centered in Him."

A Devotional Air

A praise of Glory is a soul of silence that remains like a lyre under the mysterious touch of the Holy Spirit so that He may draw from it divine harmonies; it knows that suffering is a string that produces still more beautiful sounds; so it loves to see this string on its instrument that it may more delightfully move the heart of God.

~ St. Elizabeth of the Trinity

Beloved, you are the rhythmic pulse that creates new symphonies of light within our iridescent Self. The eternal flow of Your love moves ceaselessly through each open chamber of our souls in countless ripples of luminous joy and blessedness. Although at times we may feel Your presence ebb and flow from our faculties, you remain lovingly the same, resting in your Heavenly repose, undisturbed by the influx of our temporal concerns, which can present themselves as opportunities for continuous growth if intuitively received and understood. Your essence is equally available in both shadow and light.

St. Therese of Lisieux encourages us to allow our souls the freedom to sing, dance, praise, and love. Beloved, may the celestial rhythm of your movements bring an interior lyre to the aspirations of the soul, the sweet, unheard melody that nudges us forward into the Divine mystery. Listen to the interior beat that God has placed in the nook of your soul, the ascending, voiceless rhythm that manifests the grace of God's indwelling presence. John O'Donohue writes, "When you listen with your soul, you come into rhythm and unity with the music of the universe."

God choreographs and renews the soul, clearing away the habitual debris of personal entanglement. We must allow the Beloved to lead us within the great auditorium of life. As we waltz in sacred unison, much progress will be made. The interior rhythm has no other purpose, no other aim than to elevate the soul beyond self-doubt: to joy, to bliss, to realization and peace, the radiant symmetries of our true nature, free from the egoic stamp of self-interpretation and rigid movement.

Think of Me

Let us take refuge from this world. You can do this in spirit, even if you are kept here in the body. You can at the same time be here and present to the Lord. Your soul must hold fast to him, you must follow after him in your thoughts, you must tread his ways by faith, not in outward show. You must take refuge in him. He is your refuge and your strength.

~ St. Ambrose of Milan

Take refuge in the silent repose of the Divine heart and rest easy, for God desires only what is best for the progression of your soul. Amid trial and misfortune, Her visitations of grace dispel all anxiety of self. Keep your thoughts close to God. The Lord ordered these same sentiments to St. Catherine of Sienna, saying: "Think of Me and I will think of Thee." Let our hearts find sanctuary in Him alone as we cast our devotional gaze upon the One who calls us the dearest of the dearest. St. Teresa of Avila writes, "Whenever we think of Christ we should recall the love that led him to bestow on us so many graces and favors, and also the great love God showed in giving us in Christ a pledge of his love; for love calls for love in return. Let us strive to keep this always before our eyes and to rouse ourselves to love Him. For if at some time the Lord should grant us the grace of impressing his love on our hearts, all will become easy for us and we shall accomplish great things quickly and without effort." During difficult times, may the clouds depart to reveal the hidden treasures that God seeks to bestow upon us, and may our interior gaze find its heavenly abode. St. Elizabeth of the Trinity writes, "[W]hen you feel a terrible void, think how the capacity of your soul is being enlarged so that it can receive God—becoming as it were, infinite as God is infinite." Thinking of God with the sincerity of heart draws the divine essence near to balm our wearied faculties with the nectar of infinite peace.

St. Bernard of Clairvaux writes, "The more I contemplate God, the more God looks on me. The more I pray to him, the more he thinks of me too." Give the Beloved your first and last thought of the day and in-between imitate His love. For to imitate love is to advance in love, and if anything upsets you, the soul will have its recourse with the Divine indweller who waits joyously to gladden your heart. St. Francis de Sales writes, "I want to tell you not to lose your serenity because of your imperfections, and always to have the zest to raise yourself up. It gives me joy to see each day you begin again. There is no better way to finish life well than to return to the starting point always and not ever to think that we have done enough."

The Inner Chamber

Enter the inner chamber of your mind; shut out all thoughts save that of God, and such as can aid you in seeking him; close your door and seek him. Believe me, if we neither possess nor strive to obtain this peace at home, we shall never find it abroad.

~ St. Teresa of Avila

St. Paul teaches us to pray anywhere while the Savior says, "Go into your room." But you must understand that this room is not the room with four walls that confines your body when you are in it, but the secret space within you where your thoughts are enclosed and where your sensations arrive. That is your prayer room, always with you, wherever you are, always secret, wherever you are, with your only witness being God.

St. Thomas à Kempis writes, "Christ will come to you offering His consolation, if you prepare a fit dwelling for Him in your heart, whose beauty and glory, wherein He takes delight, are all from within.

His visits with the inward man are frequent, His communion sweet and full of consolation, His peace great, and His intimacy wonderful indeed. Therefore, faithful soul, prepare your heart for this Bridegroom, that He may come and dwell within you." Enter the formless space of the heart where nothing is lacking, that little altar of veiled heaven where the perfume of love emanates through the silent repose of a reflecting heart.

St. Ambrose of Milan writes, "He enters by the open door; he has promised to come in, and he cannot deceive. Embrace him, the one you have sought; turn to him, and be enlightened; hold him fast, ask him not to go in haste, beg him not to leave you. The Word of God moves swiftly; he is not won by the lukewarm, nor held fast by the negligent. Let your soul be attentive to his word; follow carefully the path God tells you to take, for he is swift in his passing… Whoever seeks Christ in this way, and finds him, can say: I held him fast, and I will not let him go before I bring him into my mother's house, into the room of her who conceived me. What is this 'house,' this 'room,' but the deep and secret places of your heart? Maintain this house, sweep out its secret recesses until it becomes immaculate and rises as a spiritual temple for a holy priesthood, firmly secured by Christ, the cornerstone, so that the Holy Spirit may dwell in it. Whoever seeks Christ in this way, whoever prays to Christ in this way, is not abandoned by him. On the contrary, Christ comes again and again to visit such a person, for he is with us until the end of the world."

The inner room of the heart is our refuge, the interior sanctuary where the voiceless sermons of grace echo through the open manifolds of our deepest mystical chambers. Dorothy Day reminds us that Christ is always with us, always asking for room in our hearts. How could we deny such a divine guest? Meister Eckhart writes, "Be prepared at all times for the gifts of God, and be ready always for new ones. For God is a thousand times more ready to give than we are to receive." Our souls must hold fast to the truth that God desires us to have recourse with divine love, for the soul, intuitively by nature understands that beyond the horizon of self-interest and gain, heaven is formlessly revealed to gladden hearts. St. Ambrose of Milan encourages us to follow after God in our thoughts, to areas His way by faith, and to take refuge in Him. The Beloved is our refuge, hope, and strength. It is here our soul seeks its natural repose, far from the clamour of surface life.

St. Symeon Metaphrastis writes, "For the soul's will is able to preserve the body free from the vitiation of the senses, to keep the soul away from worldly distraction, and to guard the heart from scattering its thoughts into the world, completely walling them in and holding them back from base concerns and pleasures. Whenever the Lord sees someone acting in this manner, perfecting and guarding himself, disposed to serve Him with fear and trembling, He extends to Him the assistance of His grace." We are interior pilgrims, the partakers and caretakers of love. May our souls reflect the transcendental beauty of God, for there is no other purpose for our existence upon these temporal grounds. All is secondary.

Timeless Patience

We live inside a tiny moment of time. All of our time, compared with eternity, is nothing. It is a serious waste to let a day go by without allowing God to change us.

~Richard Rolle

Never think it's too late to set off in the pursuit of the Divine, for each flower blooms and produces its sweet, fragrant balm in its own time. St. Teresa of Avila writes, "If we plant a flower or a shrub and water it daily it will grow so tall that in time we shall need a spade and a hoe to uproot it." Be patient with time, because it will serve and benefit your soul well. St. Francis of Assisi reminds us that true progress quietly and persistently moves along without notice. Time, like nature, is never stagnant. Even mountains are no longer perceived as stoic and still or massive symbols of quiet endurance and immovability, for they move unseen, swaying gently upon where they rest.

St. John Paul writes, "For a stalk to grow or a flower to open there must be time that cannot be forced; nine months must go by for the birth of a human child; to write a book or compose music often years must be dedicated to patient research. To find the mystery there must be patience, interior purification, silence, waiting." Nothing truly worthwhile can be rushed. Patience and perseverance is truly a gift of grace. Each day we must arrive and allow ourselves to be loved and guided toward God's abiding presence. Louis Lallemant writes, "As time goes on, the way will gradually be rendered less rough and the difficulties will be smoothed away, because the purer our hearts become, the more abundantly we shall receive graces." Remain steadfast despite the clouds that obscure the heart, for God feels your approach and takes a joyful delight, dispelling all notions of stagnation.

St. Francis de Sales reminds us that remaining stationary for a long time is impossible. The man who makes no gain loses the little he has gained. The man who does not climb upward goes down the ladder. We must keep on keeping on. St. Thomas à Kempis writes, "Friend, don't give up your spiritual journey. You still have time. Why do you keep putting off your decision day after day? You can start immediately. You can say, 'This is the moment to start moving. Now is the time to begin the fight and then change my ways.'" Refuse to live a life consumed by the expectations of a distant future or failed past for we cannot be defined by what doesn't come to us. All we have is the present moment. Gabriela Papayannis reminds us, "Whoever lives in the future in his fantasy (or imagination) is naive, because the future belongs only to God. The Joy of Christ is found only in the present, in the Eternal Present of God." Regard not the constraints of time, but only the love that presents itself in the eternal now, for the Divine will wondrously operate in the present moment. St. Teresa of Calcutta reminds us that "Yesterday is gone. Tomorrow has not yet come. We have only today. Let us begin."

God Speaks to Souls

He desired me so I came close.
No one can near God unless He has
prepared a bed for you.
A thousand souls hear His call every
second,
but most every one then looks into their
life's mirror and
says, "I am not worthy to leave this
sadness."
When I first heard His courting song, I too
looked at all I had done in my life and said,
"How can I gaze into His omnipresent
eyes?"
I spoke those words with all my heart,
but then He sang again, a song even
sweeter,
and when I tried to shame myself once more
from His presence
God showed me His compassion and spoke
a divine truth,
"I made you, dear, and all I make is
perfect.
Please come close, for I

desire
you.

Love Poems from God *by Daniel Ladinsky.*

Our souls are intuitively perceptive and heavenly designed. Truly, we are divine thoughts in motion, reflective images of the Beloved, encased in bodily form. God communes and renders our hearts free from the debris of the egoic self. St. Louis de Blois writes, "God purifies, humbles, instructs our souls…to his will; everything defective, everything deformed, everything disagreeable to his sight, he removes from them, and at the same time embellishes them with all the ornaments which can make them pleasing in his eyes. And when he finds them faithful, full of patience and good-will; when the long endurance of tribulations has brought them, with the assistance of his grace, to such a degree of perfection that they suffer with tranquillity and joy all manner of temptation and afflictions: then he unites them not intimately to himself, confides to them his secrets and his mysteries and communicates himself to them without reserve."

God communes with souls that mirror the Divine will, souls that are void of self-gain or personal desire. Her voiceless sermon cultivates the celestial garden of our hearts. St. Elizabeth Ann Seton writes, "God dwells within. Our soul is God's palace! Conversation with him is without bounds or limits. As long as we will enter within ourselves, and as long a time as we will remain, we may enjoy this heavenly conversation in perfect liberty."

Meister Eckhart teaches us that the discovery or the recovery of our interior silence enables us to begin to listen to the ascending language of heaven, that unspeakable joy that moves undisturbed through the open manifold of a silent heart. And St. Teresa of Calcutta writes, "In nature we find silence—the trees, flowers, and grass grow in silence. The stars, the moon, and the sun move in silence. Silence of the heart is necessary so you can hear God." The Divine breathes through nature, casting beckons of light upon her emerald fields, the diverse hue of the morning light igniting nature into her full bloom.

St. Francis de Sales writes, "God displays in a marvellous manner the incomprehensible riches of his power in the vast array of things that we see in nature, but he causes the infinite treasures of his goodness to show forth in an even more magnificent way in the unparalleled variety that we see in grace. Even as birds on the wing meet the air continually, let us go where we will meet with that Presence always and everywhere." God's intelligence is omnipresent, whose qualities shimmer throughout all of nature. Jeanne Guyon writes, "As one sees a river pass into the ocean, lose itself in it, its water for a time distinguished from that of the sea, till it gradually becomes transformed into the same sea, and possesses all its qualities; so was my soul lost in God, who communicated to it His qualities."

The Divine communes with the soul in subtle waves that ebb and flow, firstly in visitations of an interior peace that is void of mental input or imaginations. A grace that unknowingly ascends upon the heart, a lightness that transcends the burdens of matter. God reciprocally inspires us to be present. We must train ourselves to listen to the eternal whisper that bellows forth its sweet odour that smooths and stills the clouded debris, enhancing our joy.

Charles Journet writes, "In times of difficulty or sadness, in times of suffering, if you frequently call to mind that God is in you to give you his love, you will not be alone, you will find the Guest within you, and he will answer you." The Divine never leaves the port of our heart despite the external waves that crash against its purest aspirations. The heart is the intuitive radio of perception, the translator and dwelling house of love, where the formless forms Her reflective image as she cleanses the mirror of our heart free from the gathered debris that has dimmed the eternal light. But God remains with us and in us, unchanged by the weight and transport of life. St. Macarius the Great reminds that the lamp of grace in the soul is always lit, giving off illumination. God seeks us to listen attentively to His gentle, unassuming voice, a language felt, an experience void of sensory input or reason. St. Teresa of Calcutta writes, "Listen in silence because if your heart is full of other things you cannot hear the voice of God." St. Benedict reminds us to listen and attend with the ear of the heart. If we seek to deepen our relationship with God, we must begin to listen in silence, for to listen is to truly see and move with vision.

Resting on Your Heart

I wish to smile, resting on Your Heart and there tell You again and again that I love You, O my Lord.

~ St. Therese of Lisieux

We must be gentle with ourselves and tend to our hearts, for therein dwells the infinite source of love and peace. The spiritual heart is enshrined with the odour of Heaven, and there we must seek out the Divine indweller. The shortest but what seems the toughest pilgrimage is only one and a half feet from the egoic mind to the heart. God wants nothing from you but the serenity of a peaceful heart, for the ordinances of quietudes are imprinted within our souls. St. Ignatius of Loyola writes, "Try to keep your soul always in peace and quiet, always ready for whatever our lord may wish to work in you." The Beloved's voiceless sermon ascends through the manifolds of a resting heart. It is there the soul seeks its repose and delight with a joyful sincerity. St. Teresa of Calcutta reminds us that God speaks in the silence of the heart by Divine grace. It is there that God seeks out our love as we seek, by Divine grace. God loves us through His love. She desires us to draw close to the Divine heart where our soul becomes enthroned by love. And from this hidden experience, not only does our interior world change, but also the way we view the exterior. Truly, a transformative union takes place beyond reason and time, bringing the invisible to the visible through subtle currents of change.

St. Josemaria Escriva writes, "Our Lord is always ready to give you the necessary grace for the new conversion you need, for that ascent in the supernatural field." Resting upon the heart isn't a motionless activity, but rather a steady motion towards the Divine, whose grace magnetically draws the advancing soul to its peaceful repose. Be tender with yourself, for the way appears without pace or quickness of breath, for everything ripens within its own time. We must persevere joyously along the path, despite the tumult of life that seeks to weigh upon the soul's aspiration for union with its Beloved. Don't be anchored by a temporal life or accept its transports, for Divine love is borderless, free from sensory restriction. Padre Pio reminds us not to let the sad sight of human injustice sadden your soul. We must make our hearts a hermitage, a sanctuary of repose that emanates a serenity free from the world's slaving glare for the Beloved to reveal His essence.

Spirit reveals Her Grace through the conduct of a peaceful repose when the breath is no longer claimed by the weight of the sense faculties, as energy withdraws into the depths of the soul, where love dwells far from the reach of reason. Only therein do we find true reflective rest.

ABOUT THE AUTHOR

Conor McCourt was born and raised during the conflict in the North of Ireland in the historical city of Armagh where St. Patrick built his great stone church in 445AD, making Armagh the ecclesiastical capital also known as the Christian capital of Ireland and centre of Christianity in Ireland. Armagh was also the birthplace of the 11th-century Saint Malachy who was born only a ten-minute walk from McCourt's home; his city is so steeped in religious and cultural treasures that the older he gets newfound respect grows for what rests at his door.

As a child he was always inquisitive when it came to spiritual matters. His Mum and her friends would often clean the local St. Patrick's Cathedral, so he thought there was no better time or setting to ask questions about God and the unexplained mysteries. His mother would make him polish the seats more rigorously—while he avoided the swirling bats above—but maybe she was teaching him early on to seek answers in silence. In time, it would prove to be his greatest friend, for stillness and silence was the key for Spirit to reveal Grace upon an inquisitive heart like his.

Growing up, he felt what he could best describe as an internal nudge to know more. Somehow, he felt guided from an early age, even through his teenage rebellious years. He felt that central drawing, although, he couldn't understand the feeling. Over the past twenty-five years, his spiritual practice has developed through God's Grace and his perseverance to continue his journey despite the many challenges and responsibilities he has in life. This proves that anyone, no matter their personal environment or circumstances, can have a deeper connection and continuous relationship with God.

RESOURCES

à Kempis, Thomas, 2004. *Consolations for My Soul*, translated by William Griffin. Crossroad.

à Kempis, Thomas, 1878. *Of the Imitation of Christ.* London: Chapman and Hall.

Carter, T.T., 1903. *Spiritual Instructions on the Holy Eucharist in The Inheritance of the Saints* London.

de Sales, Saint Francis, 2017. *Consoling Thoughts of Saint Francis de Sales*, compiled by Pere Huget. Ivory Falls Books.

de Sales, Saint Francis, 1972. *Introduction to the Devout Life*, translated by John K. Ryan. New York: Image Books.

Hillesum, Etty, 1996. *An Interrupted Life: The Diaries, 1941-1943 and Letters from Westerbork,* translated by Arnold J. Pomerans. New York: Henry Holt and Company.

Love Poems from God, translated by Daniel Ladinsky Penguin Books, 1999.

Manning, Henry Edward, 1850. *Sermons in the Inheritance of the Saints* London.

Merton, Thomas, 1961. *New Seeds of Contemplation,* Boston: Shambala Publications, Inc.

Merton, Thomas, 1992. *The Springs of Contemplation*, New York: Farrar, Straus, Giroux.

Nouwen, Henri J.M., 1986. *Reaching Out: The Three Movements of the Spiritual Life*, New York: Image Books.

Pusey, E.B, 1903. *Parochial Sermons in the Inheritance of the Saints*, London .

Rahner, Karl, 1968. *Everyday Faith*, Herder and Herder.

Excerpt of *Whispers from the Sanctuary* by Conor McCourt

Day 3

Morning

The Celestial Explorer

When we feel uplifted in Spirit's presence, an urgency floods our heart to seek for infinitely more. We experience moments of deepening awareness. Look back over your journey to that first feeling of wonderment and reflect how far you have travelled over what seemed mostly mountainous terrain. The spiritual life is not about being in a permanent state of positivity, it can be raw, lonely, and sensitive. Saint Ignatius of Loyola writes "A man who finds the path to virtue difficult yet sets out on it bravely to conquer himself." Despite all difficulties, how blessed is the life that feels without seeing and whose faith abides in the joyous calmness of heart.

MORNING REFLECTIONS

Rest easy and immerse yourself in the thought of God. May the internal whispers of your love reach the receptive shore of Spirit, for here dwells the source and most joyous existence to all brave conquering souls.

Contemplative prayer is the pure, loving gaze that finds God everywhere. ~ Brother Lawrence

The presence of God calms the soul and gives it quiet and repose. ~ François Fénèlon

PERSONAL COMMENTARY

On my spiritual path, I've often felt alone, isolated, a kind of an outsider at times looking in. The strange paradox is that I have never felt loneliness, but instead an interior friendship forming under the veil of the external world. At times I've been misunderstood and misjudged; I feel a lot of readers can fathom these very normal feelings. All these things would make anyone feel more excluded, alone, and further from God, but these mental commentaries come from misplaced minds which cannot envision more to life beyond the horizon of their mental environment. Despite this, it fuelled me more stubbornly to seek the Eternal guide of my heart, for who really can interpret another's experience of faith when it comes to the great Divine romance with God? The interior path back home is privately between soul and spirit and perfectly unique for everyone, yet the subtle vibration of interior Love magnetically draws all souls back to the central core by the medium of Grace. The soul seeks by its nature to be alone with its celestial companion, a loneliness void of sadness, unworthiness, or the feeling of abandonment. Our soul longs to be alone with Spirit, for in our aloneness we become spiritualized by the aloneness of Love.

Evening

Seeing God in All

There is a little story about a man who, in desperation, called out to God, "Let me see you," and a star shined brightly, but the man did not see. The man shouted, "God show me a miracle," and a baby was born, but the man did not notice. So, the man cried out in despair, "Touch me God and let me know you are here," where upon God reached down and touched the man, but the man brushed the butterfly away from his shoulder and walked on. As time goes by in our spiritual journey, we will intuitively realize there is no place where God is not. He is in the breeze that cools, in the sun that warms the body and gives needed nutrients He calls through the sweet song from a morning bird. He is in the friend that advises and comforts; he is in the smile of recognition from a stranger's eyes. St. Francis de Sale reminds us, "God is in all things and in all places. There is no place or thing in this world where God is not truly present. Just as where birds fly, they always encounter the air, so also wherever we go or wherever we are, we find ourselves in God's presence."

EVENING REFLECTIONS

Behind every form is the formless hidden essence of Spirit, we are all portable pieces of Heaven with hidden rooms of celestial treasures that seek a cheerful glance.

Finding God in all things. ~ Saint Ignatius of Loyola

A fish cannot drown in water,
A bird does not fall in air.
In the fire of creation,
God doesn't vanish:
The fire brightens.
Each creature God made

must live in its own true nature;
How could I resist my nature,
That lives for oneness with God?
~ Mechthild of Magdeburg

Whispers of the Sanctuary can be purchased from book retailers or directly from the publisher at books.gracepointpublishing.com.

BE A PART OF OUR ONLINE COMMUNITY

Facebook groups:

Contemplative Soul: A shared space for individuals that seek an interior awareness of God's indwelling presence.

https://www.facebook.com/centeringsoul75/

Soul Whispers: A sacred place for spiritual seekers, lovers of God, for inspiration from saintly souls, mystics, poets, and storytellers. All faith traditions are welcome.

https://www.facebook.com/groups/267021457954312

Friends of Whispers from the Sanctuary: Small excerpts from the book will be shared and similar-based Christian contemplative wisdom from the many Mystics, Saints, and storytellers.

https://www.facebook.com/groups/665460161862785

For more great books from GraceLight Press

Visit Books.GracePointPublishing.com

If you enjoyed reading *Gazing Upon Eternity,* and purchased it through an online retailer, please return to the site and write a review to help others find the book.

Printed in Great Britain
by Amazon